Der...

The Lament for Arthur ...
The Holy Ground, Blinded by the Light

The Lament for Arthur Cleary: 'Bolger captures and articulates the changeling spirit of Irish society – Dublin's in particular – and he does so more accurately, poignantly and amusingly than anything seen on stage in recent years. The eyes, ears and voice of a fine poet haven't failed him and he translates his acute observation of today's young and old into the language of theatre with an inventive ease which any of our most celebrated playwrights might envy. This is a play of our times, expertly presented, a beautiful articulation of the dread with which city people watch the relentless encroachment of decay and corruption in the name of progress.' *Sunday Independent*

In High Germany: 'A powerful and moving evocation of the reality of Ireland's production of the "young Europeans".' *Irish Independent*

The Holy Ground: 'Bolger's bitter, touching monologue . . ,'[is] the best, saddest one-acter on offer this year, finely-crafted in its language, admirable in intention, and in its closing moments a work of elegiac poetry which should be seen by all.' *Sunday Tribune*

Blinded by the Light: 'Hysterically funny, its wild humour always on the edge of dementia. It is in many ways a parable of Ireland's referenda years, the years in which the notion of private conscience became impossible, the years of the undermining of that wonderful right defined by the American Supreme Court as "the right to be left alone" . . . The comedy is freewheeling, absurd, associative, handled with immense skill and wit by an author whose taste in bad taste is impeccable. It zig-zags between theatre of the absurd and kitchen comedy, between farce and social realism in ways that are always highly entertaining.' *Irish Times*

Dermot Bolger was born in Finglas, North Dublin, in 1959. He founded the Raven Arts Press in 1977 while still at school and has since been a major force at the cutting edge of Irish writing as a playwright, novelist, poet and editor. His eight plays, including *The Lament for Arthur Cleary*, *In High Germany* and *The Passion of Jerome*, have received the Samuel Beckett Award, two Edinburgh Fringe Firsts, the BBC Stewart Parker Prize and the O.Z. Whitehead Award. In 1997 he was Playwright-in-Association with the Abbey Theatre in Dublin. His seven novels, including *The Journey Home*, *A Second Life*, *Father's Music* and *Temptation* have received the A.E. Memorial Prize and Macauley Fellowship and been translated into many languages. He also originated and edited the best-selling *Finbar's Hotel* collaborative novels.

DERMOT BOLGER

Plays: 1

The Lament for Arthur Cleary
In High Germany
The Holy Ground
Blinded by the Light

Introduced by Fintan O'Toole

Methuen Drama

METHUEN CONTEMPORARY DRAMATISTS

1 3 5 7 9 10 8 6 4 2

This collection first published in the United Kingdom in 2000 by
Methuen Publishing Limited
215 Vauxhall Bridge Road, London SW1V 1EJ

An early version of *The Lament for Arthur Cleary* was first published
in the United Kingdom by Nick Hern Books in 1990 in an anthology
entitled *The Crack in the Emerald*
In High Germany and *The Holy Ground* first published
together with *The Lament for Arthur Cleary* and *One Last White Horse*
in 1992 by Penguin Books in a volume entitled *A Dublin Quartet*
The Lament for Arthur Cleary, *In High Germany* and *The Holy Ground*
copyright © 1990, 1992, 2000 by Dermot Bolger
Blinded by the Light first published in 1997 jointly by New Island Books in
Ireland and Nick Hern Books in the United Kingdom
in a volume together with *April Bright*
Copyright © 1997, 2000

Collection copyright © 2000 by Dermot Bolger
Introduction copyright © 1992, 2000 by Fintan O'Toole

Methuen Publishing Limited Reg. No. 3543167

A CIP catalogue record for this book is available from the British Library

ISBN 0 413 74500 7

Typeset by Deltatype Ltd, Birkenhead
Printed and bound in Great Britain by Cox & Wyman Ltd, Reading, Berks

Caution

Contents

For David Byrne

Dermot Bolger
Chronology

1977 Founded Raven Arts Press. Editor until 1992
1980 *The Habit of Flesh*, poems, published by Raven
      Arts Press
1981 *Finglas Lilies*, poems, published by Raven Arts
      Press
1982 *No Waiting America*, poems, published by Raven
      Arts Press
1985 First novel, *Night Shift*, published by Brandon
      Publishers; reissued Penguin, 1992; received
      A.E. Memorial Prize
1986 *Internal Exiles*, poems, published by Dolmen Press
1987 *The Woman's Daughter*, novel, published by Raven
      Arts Press; received Macaulay Fellowship and
      Sunday Tribune Arts Award, shortlisted Hughes
      Fiction Prize
      The Bright Wave: An Tonn Gheal (editor) published
      by Raven Arts Press; received An Duais Bhord
      Na Gaelige
1989 *The Lament for Arthur Cleary* staged by Wet Paint
      Arts, Dublin; received Samuel Beckett Prize,
      Edinburgh Fringe First Award, BBC Stewart
      Parker Prize
      Leinster Street Ghosts, poems, published by Raven
      Arts Press
1990 *Blinded by the Light* staged by the Abbey Theatre
      on their Peacock stage; received the O.Z.
      Whitehead Prize and Listoinel Prize
      In High Germany staged by the Gate Theatre,
      Dublin; also filmed by RTE Television
      The Holy Ground staged by the Gate Theatre,
      Dublin; received Edinburgh Fringe First Award
      The Journey Home, novel, published by Penguin
      Books; short-listed for the *Irish Times*/Aer Lingus
      Irish Literature Prize and Hughes Fiction Prize

1991   *One Last White Horse* staged by the Abbey
       Theatre on their Peacock stage
       Invisible Dublin: A Journey Through Dublin's Suburbs
       (editor) published by Raven Arts Press
       The Woman's Daughter, extended version,
       published by Penguin Books
1992   *Emily's Shoes*, novel, published by Penguin Books
       Co-founded New Island Books
       Selected Poems of Francis Ledgwidge (editor)
       published by New Island Books
1993   *The Picador Book of Contemporary Irish Fiction*
       (editor) published by Picador
1994   *A Second Life*, novel, published by Penguin Books
       A Dublin Bloom, stage adaptation of *Ulysses*,
       staged by Rosenbach Library, Philadelphia
1995   *April Bright* staged by the Abbey Theatre on
       their Peacock stage
       The Vintage Book of Contemporary Irish Fiction
       published in New York by Vintage Books
1996   *Edward No Hands*, television play (RTE/BBC co-
       production)
1997   *Father's Music*, novel, published by Flamingo/
       HarperCollins
       Finbar's Hotel, collaborative novel, published by
       Picador/New Island Books
       Playwright-in-Association at the Abbey Theatre,
       Dublin
1998   *Taking My Letters Back, New and Selected Poems*,
       published by New Island Books
1999   *The Passion of Jerome* staged by the Abbey
       Theatre on their Peacock stage
       Ladies' Night at Finbar's Hotel, collaborative novel
       (editor), published by Picador/New Island Books
2000   *Consenting Adults* staged by Fishamble Theatre
       Company, Dublin
       Temptation, novel, published by Flamingo/
       HarperCollins
       The New Picador Book of Contemporary Irish Fiction
       (editor) published by Picador

Introduction
On The Frontier

Dublin, in the late 1980s and early 1990s, was a frontier town, on the edge of Europe, on the fringes of the Irish nation, at the end of its tether. The city seemed to exist largely at its own extremes. In the previous thirty years, it had ceased to be the teeming, intense and intimate city that James Joyce and Sean O'Casey mythologised and become raw and sprawling, an awkward adolescent spreading its limbs over old villages, through lush farmland, up the sides of hills. As the old inner city – the city whose ironies of classical architecture inhabited by class-ridden poverty created the bitter humour of its people – had become gap-toothed with dereliction, so the new suburbs had been voraciously eating up the surrounding countryside. New places had been born, places without history, without the accumulated resonances of centuries, places that prefigured the end of the fierce notion of Irishness that had sustained the state for seventy years. Sex and drugs and rock 'n' roll were more important in the new places than the old Irish totems of Land, Nationality and Catholicism. Dermot Bolger comes from one of these places, the working-class suburb of Finglas to the north of the city, and his work is marked by this fact.

The loss of a sense of history is also a liberation from the shackles of the past. Joyce's Stephen Dedalus regarded history as a nightmare from which he was trying to awake, but in the suburbs that nightmare is buried beneath concrete and tarmac. The juggernauts whizzing by on the motorway carry not the burden of history but goods for export from the Most Profitable Location in Europe for American Industry, as the ads in *Time* magazine call the new Ireland. The great tradition of Irish writing is silent on the subject of suburbs, so you can slip out from under its shadow. No one has ever mythologised this housing estate, this footbridge over the motorway, that video rental shop. It is, for the writer, virgin territory.

A loss, though, is still a loss. We need to shape our lives with some sense of significance, some notion of a journey that ties together past, present and future. If history is not given to us, we need to invent it, to create personal histories, to map out private journeys. This is not the sense of loss that creates nostalgia, of which there is hardly a trace in Dermot Bolger's plays, but the sense of loss that creates a hole that must be filled. The liberation from the past is physically present in these plays, in their formal adventurousness, their deeply European character, the search in their language for a poetry of the unpoetic, the everyday. But if the liberation creates the framework for these plays, the loss creates the hunger that drives their characters. Their restlessness, their need to undertake voyages, their search for a vaguely discerned home, all come from a feeling that something has been misplaced and cannot be found again. In these plays you can go back but you can never return; you can seek but you can never find.

If you see yourself as being in a tradition, as part of a historic story that is still playing itself out, then you are not free to step outside that story, rewrite bits of the plot, remember the language of the early scenes, invent new endings. Belonging to no obvious tradition, either in a literary sense or in the wider sense of being part of a traditional Ireland, Dermot Bolger is free to do precisely these things, and that freedom helps to shape these plays. Two apparently fixed and sacred aspects of the Irish tradition are the Gaelic language, with its languid and sorrowful literature, and Catholicism. Both seem very far in time and place from the world of Dermot Bolger's plays, yet precisely because of that distance both are available to him to shape in his own way, to bend to the inflections of his own accent.

The Lament for Arthur Cleary is inspired by one of the

most famous poems in the Gaelic language, 'Caoineadh
Airt Ui Laoire', a lament for a man who dies because
he cannot bend his pride to the demands of oppressive
English rule, cannot understand that the Ireland he left
to go and fight on the Continent has, on his return,
become a more dangerous place. *The Holy Ground*, less
obviously, draws on a great Gaelic love poem in which
the writer complains that his love has stolen God away
from him. But in both cases the Gaelic sources are used
not to place the plays in an unbroken tradition but to
suggest parallels between Ireland now, fractured and
confused as it is, and the broken, dissolving, powerfully
angry world of the last days of a dying Gaelic
civilisation. It is not an unbroken tradition but a
tradition of *being broken* that is at issue. If there is a
history at work, it is a history of one world giving way
painfully to another, just as in the suburbs of Dublin
one world is giving way to another one, more uncertain
but less confined.

The sense of things dead or dying is everywhere in
the plays. In *The Lament for Arthur Cleary* the central
character is already dead, and the play itself is enacted
on the borders of death and life. Heroin, the death-
bringer, the suburban Nemesis of our times, is a
principal actor in the play, an image both of a dying
Dublin and of the radical openness of the new city,
willing to embrace anything that is going, innocent and
raw and wild and vulnerable enough in the early 1980s
to become, for a time, the heroin capital of Europe. In
Blinded by the Light, one of the sacred images of national
resistance and Catholic martyrdom, the preserved head
of Blessed (now Saint) Oliver Plunkett, executed by the
English as a Papist traitor, is at the centre of the play's
increasingly surreal comedy, becoming the obscure object
of a young man's desperate desires. And, in less
dramatic ways, other deaths – the death of a husband,
the death of a father – hang over the two shorter plays
in this volume.

This concentration on death, though, should also alert
us to the spiritual quest that is being undertaken in these
plays. The second element of the Irish past that emerges
here is Catholicism, and it is revived in strange ways.
Bolger's plays have been rightly praised for their realism,
for the way in which they reflect, and reflect on, a
changed set of social circumstances. But it must be
remembered that Irish reality itself remains deeply
imbued with an often surreal religiosity. There is again a
paradox: one of the ways you knew that traditional
Ireland was breaking down in the 1980s was the
resurgence of a despairing, bitter Catholicism, manifested
in everything from the insertion of a clause into the Irish
Constitution prohibiting abortion in 1983 to the defeat
of an attempt to permit divorce in 1986 and to the
crowds who gathered in fields or churchyards on
summer evenings to watch statues of the Blessed Virgin
waving, dancing and weeping. This too was social
reality, however surreal, and Dermot Bolger has not
been afraid to engage with it in his work.

The world of Dermot Bolger's plays is godless, but it
is not irreligious. The complaint of a woman who has
just buried her husband that the dead man, with his
almost psychotic fanaticism, stole her Christ from her is
the key to this world from which God is absent, but the
need, the search, for some other God cannot be
avoided. The terraces of German football stadiums
during the European Championship become the site for
a sort of Mass at which the congregation of the Irish
diaspora offers the only prayer to the vanished God that
it can muster: the chant 'IRELAND, IRELAND,
IRELAND'. The border guards who bar the way on
Arthur Cleary's voyage are also angels guarding the
gates of Heaven or Hell.

Because Irish reality has become increasingly surreal,
the usual division in writing between the realist on the
one hand and the fantasist on the other has begun to
break down. Realism has to become surrealism;

naturalism has to become supernaturalism. Dermot
Bolger's work is at the forefront of this development. On
the one hand, he deals with areas of Irish reality that
have largely been avoided by the theatre heretofore:
modern urban life, the new, shifting, unsentimental
emigration, the plague of heroin, the realities of poverty
at the uneasy edge of the European Community. He is,
in that sense, a realistic writer, counterposing a new
grasp of what it is like to live in urban Ireland now to
the old pieties of place and character and landscape. On
the other hand, though, his realism is not naturalistic.
These plays are not descriptions of a world; they are
forays into it. They reflect the world they inhabit just as
the steamed-up window of a bus reflects the face of a
child drawing pictures on it, an image that is used in
another of Bolger's plays, *One Last White Horse*. The face
is real; the setting is resolutely downbeat; but the image
that is reflected has its own surreal logic, and the
pictures that are drawn on it are the cyphers of the
imagination.

The weakness of much of social realism in the theatre
has always been its refusal to accept that dreams,
fantasies, the products of the imagination are not escapes
from everyday reality but integral parts of that reality.
Ireland itself is the product of dreams – the dreams of
Independence first, then the dreams of modernity, the
American dreams of high-tech foreigners coming to
make all the failures right. And in these plays the
dreams come in waves: the political dreams, the dream-
worlds of soccer and television, the dreams of family, of
recapturing a lost time, the imagined children who
animate Monica's life in *The Holy Ground*. Both of the
full-length plays have this overwhelmingly dream-like
quality without ever giving way to the obscurity and self-
indulgence that dreams can be a licence for.

Ireland, it should be remembered, is a country
described by the dominant political figure of the 1980s
and early 1990s, the Taoiseach (Prime Minister) Charles

Haughey, who was, as we now know, in the pay of
wealthy businessmen, as 'a dream which has yet to be
fulfilled'. When a real place is seen even by those who
run it as a dream, then real people are left with dreams,
aspirations, fantasies to live on. In *Blinded by the Light*,
Ireland has shrunk to the temporary, shabby, shifting
bedsit of a young man on the edge. Arthur Cleary's
Ireland is ground that has shifted, already a place of the
memory. Eoin's Ireland is a temporary vision conjured
up on the terraces of a foreign stadium by eleven men
in green jerseys, a vision as evanescent as any moving
statue. Monica's Ireland is a picture of another woman's
child sent in a letter home from a foreign country.
These are stateless persons, undocumented aliens in their
own country, unable to know their place because their
place has become unknowable. They are the state of a
nation.

    But they are more than that, too. The very
restlessness, the shifting, open, unformed nature of the
world of these plays, makes them also European. Here
we have not just an unofficial Ireland but also an
unofficial Europe, the Europe of the *Gastarbeiter* and the
long-haul truck driver, the Europe of the football
hooligan and the border guard. The people of these
plays abolished the borders long ago, driven to do so by
both economic and spiritual needs. In the common
European house they squat in the lower storeys. Unlike
the more settled residents, they are forced to live in
Europe, to cross its borders and follow its shifts, to
negotiate it rather than merely to occupy a fixed place
within it. If they belong anywhere, these plays belong to
the Europe that is now stretching itself untidily from
Connemara to the Caucasus, trying to find a
comfortable place to lay its increasingly uneasy head.

Fintan O'Toole
2000

The Lament for Arthur Cleary

a play in two acts

Characters

Arthur Cleary, *a Dubliner, aged thirty-five*
Kathy, *his girlfriend, aged eighteen*
Frontier Guard ⎫
Porter   ⎬ *all of whom play a variety of*
Friend   ⎭ *interchanging roles*

The Lament for Arthur Cleary was first performed by Wet Paint Arts as part of the Dublin Theatre Festival at the Project Arts Centre on 18 September 1989. The cast was as follows:

Arthur Cleary	Brendan Laird
Kathy	Hilary Fannin
Frontier Guard	Owen Roe
Porter	Berts Folan
Friend	Lynn Cahill

Directed by David Byrne
Designed by Ned McLoughlin
Music by Gerard Grennell

Act One

*As the first strains of music begin the actors file slowly on stage. The **Friend**, the **Frontier Guard** and the **Porter** in that order stand at the back of the stage with sticks in their hands, **Arthur Cleary** sits on a small box to stage right and **Kathy** takes centre stage. There is a long thin wooden platform on stage and a barrel at the far right where the **Friend** stands. When **Kathy** begins to recite her voice is echoed by a recording of itself over the music which grows in tempo.*

Kathy

My lament for you Arthur Cleary
As you lay down that crooked back lane
Under the stern wall of a factory
Where moss and crippled flowers cling.

I cupped your face in my palms
To taste life draining from your lips
And you died attempting to smile
As defiant and proud as you had lived.

*Stage goes to blackout. Over the music comes a sharp banging of sticks on the drum and the walls. They grow in fury until drowned by the climaxing soundtrack. In the sudden silence and growing dim light we discern the three figures each holding a death mask over their face and standing poised with sticks raised. As each one speaks they slowly converge on **Arthur** who now lies with **Kathy** sleeping uneasily under a white cloth beside the box. Each sentence is accompanied by a sharp thud of a stick.*

Porter (*resigned*) It's dead Arthur, don't you know it's dead?

Friend (*defiant*) When did we ever care about them son? When did we ever?

Frontier Guard (*menacingly*) Decide Arthur. With me or against me.

Friend (*spiteful*)   You'd go off with him, that old cripple.

They advance more, chanting phrases from their sentences which become jumbled into each other, their sticks making several sharp bangs which unnerve **Arthur***, the* **Porter** *laughing mockingly. They gather behind* **Arthur** *and after one final thud, they raise their sticks in a fan behind his back.* **Kathy** *wakes and sits bolt upright, the sheet clutched protectively against her.* **Arthur** *sits up too, soothing her.*

Arthur   A bad dream love, just a bad dream.

Kathy *looks at him, coming to her senses.*

Kathy   I'm frightened Arthur. I dreamt it again.

Arthur   The same one? Can you remember it?

Kathy   No, but it was the same one. It's always gone when I wake but I know it. I know the fear in it. Like the fear of nothing else. (*Pause.*) Let's go Arthur, now while we've still time.

Arthur (*half amused/half soothing*)   Go away? Listen love, I've finally come home. This is our home. Nobody can take it from us. Home. Say it.

Kathy (*nervously*)   Home?

Arthur (*firmly*)   Home.

Kathy (*less tentatively*)   Home.

Arthur (*firmly*)   Home.

His arm nestling her head, they lie back slowly as lights go to blackout.

Arthur *and* **Kathy** (*firmly*)   Home.

A new music begins, unsettling, overlaid with the sound of train wheels. A spotlight switches on, held by the **Frontier Guard***. It flickers over the stage.*

Frontier Guard   Check the wheels!

Porter For what?

Frontier Guard (*dismissively*) Just do it!

From behind the raised platform the **Porter** *switches on his torch. He keeps moving the beam up and down the wooden bars in front of which* **Arthur** *now stands in semi-darkness with a passport in his hand.* **Frontier Guard** *approaches.*

Frontier Guard Passport please.

Arthur (*turning*) Oh, sorry.

He hands him the passport which the **Frontier Guard** *examines.*

Frontier Guard Ah Irish. Irish. Boom-boom! eh! (*He laughs.*)

Arthur Yeah. Boom-bleeding-boom.

Frontier Guard *hands him back the passport.*

Frontier Guard *and* **Porter** (*ironically as they circle with torches*)
We are green, we are white,
We are Irish dynamite!

Arthur Eh, do you mind me asking? Where am I now? Which side of the border am I on?

Frontier Guard (*stops and shrugs his shoulders*) What difference to you Irish? I see you people every day, you're going this way, you're going that way, but never home. Either way you're a long way from there.

Arthur (*nods his head towards the* **Porter**) What's he looking at the wheels for?

Frontier Guard Looking for? It is the rules Irish. He does what he is told. You ordered him to look for a snowball in a fire he would sit staring all night. (**Frontier Guard** *laughs, watching the flickering beam, then turns abruptly.*) We will go on soon.

He exits as the **Porter** *closes in on* **Arthur**, *still shining the torch up and down.*

Arthur   What difference does it make? (*He looks up and down.*) Another limbo of tracks and warehouses. Could be anywhere. (*He gives a half laugh.*) Except home.

Porter (*shining the torch directly at his face*)   How can you leave a place when you're carrying it round inside you, Arthur? And how can you go back? Because after a time you can only go there in your mind. Because when you go back you can feel . . . the distance, eh. The big town just a squalid village, the big man . . . what's that you call him . . . a crock of shit. You say nothing, but you know and . . . wait till you see Arthur . . . the big men, the bosses, they know you know.

Arthur (*staring at him in astonishment*)   How do you know my name? I don't know you?

Porter   You don't know nothing.

He switches his torch off, scurrying upstage to set up the wooden box. The **Friend** *strides forward confidently towards the box. The other four characters gather behind her and begin clapping. The* **Friend** *clears her throat and then silences the others with a sweep of her hand. She stares out. There is applause scattered throughout her speech, which she halts with her hand.*

Friend (*in smooth politician's voice*)   Although we are a small nation in this great community, our heritage abounds with saints, with poets, with dreamers. But we in government are realists, first and foremost. We know we cannot all live in this one island. But we are not ashamed. Young people are to Ireland what champagne is to France! Our finest crop, the cream of our youth, nurtured from birth, raised with tender love by our young state, brought to ripeness and then plucked! For export to your factories and offices. Fellow European ministers we are but a small land with a small role to play in this great union of nations. But a land with a great history. Long before Columbus set sail in 1492, long before Amerigo Vespucci gave his name to that great continent, (*Applause takes on rhythmic effect.*) our missionaries in their boats of animal hide had already discovered the New World. Through all of the Dark Ages we have gone forth to spread the word of God among you, (*Others bless themselves.*) to petition you for arms to repel our invader, (*Others join hands and grimace.*) to fight your wars. Once more we entrust to you the flower of our youth, not black –

Cast   Oh no –

Friend   Or yellow –

Cast   Oh no –

Friend   But white –

Cast   Oh yes –

Friend   Not illiterate –

Cast   Oh no –

Friend   Or backward –

Cast   Oh no –

Friend   But qualified –

Cast   Oh yes –

Friend   Not migrants –

Cast   Oh no –

Friend   Or illegals –

Cast   Oh no –

Friend   But as equal Europeans.

There is great applause from the cast.

Friend   We know they are ready to take their place, we know you will not turn your back on them. (*Slight* *pause.*) And now my fellow minister will give a brief discourse on night life in Dublin. Thank you.

She steps down and the **Porter** *swings her around towards* **Kathy***. Both girls begin to dance their way to the back of the stage to the dance beat which grows louder. The* **Porter** *lifts the box to one side then crosses the stage in a slightly drunken fashion. The* **Frontier Guard** *clicks his fingers, checks his suit and stands self-importantly beside the raised platform as the stage is flooded with speckled light suggesting a night-club. The girls check their make-up, miming a conversation between themselves. The* **Frontier Guard** *is self-assured, leaning against the platform as though blocking a doorway, aware of his strength. The* **Porter** *approaches nervously and stops.* **Frontier Guard** *ignores him.* **Porter** *moves closer.*

Porter   What's it like inside, mister?

The **Frontier Guard** *speaks slowly as if to a child but also like a seedy doorman.*

Frontier Guard   Everything you ever dreamt of. Girls hot for it, lining the walls, leather mini-skirts, thighs like long stalks of barley waiting to be harvested.

Porter   It's that good, is it?

Frontier Guard   It's better.

Porter   So, eh, I suppose . . . is there . . . eh, any chance . . . ?

Frontier Guard   Ever hear of Matt Talbot's first miracle?

Porter   Eh, no.

Frontier Guard   Brothers they were, out in Ballybough. Three of them. Dockers. Down the kips in Monto every weekend. All three of them contracted it. (*Pause.*) The pox! Worst dose imaginable. Only one cure you know. (*He raises two fingers to form a scissors and makes a cut down at* **Porter**'s *zip. The* **Porter** *jumps back.*) The worker saint Matt Talbot was their only hope. He says

to them 'go down to the Liffey before dawn every
morning for a week, strip naked, cover yourselves in
muck and beg God for forgiveness.'

Porter   And were they cured?

Frontier Guard (*tone changing as he advances*)   No! And
the first miracle of Matt Talbot was that they didn't
murder the little runt afterwards. And it would take a
second bloody miracle by him to get the likes of you in
here. So get the hell away from this door!

Arthur *approaches, watching the* **Porter** *back off. He looks at
the* **Frontier Guard** *who shrugs his shoulders.*

Frontier Guard   Kids! Think they own the world
after one pint of beer. You looking for something?

Arthur *looks over* **Frontier Guard***'s head, as if tracing a
vanished outline.*

Arthur   A fish used to be there.

Frontier Guard   So were the Vikings.

Arthur (*pointing*)   No, you can still see the outline of the
sign.

Frontier Guard (*looking up*)   Jaysus you can too. That
wasn't today or yesterday.

Arthur   The Rock Salmon Club. Used to be my
regular. Great bands, poxy name.

Frontier Guard   Yeah, I remember it. That was what
. . . God, it's closed over ten years now. Went there a
few times meself. Never thought I'd wind up working on
the door. I was barred from it often enough. You know
yourself.

Arthur   Will you stop? I'd my skull busted in here
once. They closed the gaff for a while after. What's it
now?

Frontier Guard   Bop de bop bop around the

handbags. Under-twelves with adults. Have you been away or what?

Arthur   Yeah. For too long. I thought this place might be the same.

Frontier Guard   Just kids now, dance beat. You're welcome to have a look.

Arthur   Naw, you're all right. Thanks anyway. I'll see you around.

Frontier Guard   Yeah, good luck. (*Looks past the retreating* **Arthur** *at the girls who approach.*) Ah, here we go, the terrible twins.

The girls stop, seeing him there.

Kathy   Oh God, it's him. Not here, Sharon. Let's go somewhere else.

Friend   Where then?

Kathy   Anywhere. I hate him.

Friend   Just be nice to him, only takes a minute and you're in. You rub him up wrong.

Kathy (*shudders*)   It's him rubbing me up I hate.

Friend   So listen, what are our choices, what do you fancy doing? Stand around the streets all night . . .

The **Porter** *passes and leers at her.*

Friend   . . . get a bus home, sit with your da, take up knitting . . .

Kathy   All right, but you first.

Friend (*warning her*)   And you keep your trap shut, do you hear. You get us in enough bloody trouble.

They approach the **Frontier Guard**.

Frontier Guard   Well, girls. Anything I can do for you? Suggestions? Requests?

Friend You couldn't try letting us in for a change, Frank?

Frontier Guard I might have to frisk you girls first. Need to protect my punters.

Friend You're not the only night-club in this street.

Frontier Guard The only one that serves under-twelves like you. Does your da know you're out . . . wearing that? So how about it . . . one kiss?

*The **Porter**, in another behavioural mode, queues again behind* **Kathy**. *The **Friend** looks back at him.*

Friend Your boyfriend might get jealous. Come on, Frank, please, it's cold.

Frontier Guard You could try wearing clothes . . . those skimpy things, flaunting yourselves. No, I'd have a moral objection.

Friend Come on, Frank, please.

Frontier Guard The Brownies' meeting is over, girls. Past your bedtime.

Friend You know us, Frank, you let us in last week. We even have comps. We got them in the pub.

Frontier Guard How's your little moody friend tonight. Still stuck up? (*To **Kathy**.*) So do you call that a dress or an undress?

Kathy I see why they call them monkey suits.

Frontier Guard *looks past her at the* **Porter** *who grins.*

Frontier Guard What do you want Chink? You'll find no seagulls to put in your curry here. Try Dollymount Strand. Go on.

Porter (*oriental accent*) I just want to dance. What's it to you?

Frontier Guard Come up here, and we'll see if

you're as yellow as your skin. Back to your own country, boy.

Porter   I was born here.

Frontier Guard (*tone quieter*)   Come here a second, sonny, I won't hurt you.

Porter *approaches.*

Porter   What?

Frontier Guard *flicks him around and twists his arm behind his back.*

Frontier Guard   You weren't born anywhere. You were hatched out in the sun.

He shoves him and **Porter** *stumbles away.*

Frontier Guard   Well, girls. . . ?

Kathy   Bastard.

Friend (*hissing at her*)   Shut up. (*To* **Frontier Guard**.) Frank, come on, we've. . .

Frontier Guard (*snaps*)   Get out of my sight. Now!

Friend   Apologise to Frank.

Kathy   I will not.

Girls back away arguing as **Arthur** *approaches.* **Frontier Guard** *turns.*

Frontier Guard   You back again?

Arthur   I'll take you up on that offer.

Frontier Guard   What offer?

Arthur   See the gaff . . . memories.

Frontier Guard *shrugs his shoulders.*

Frontier Guard   Ah, listen, I've had second thoughts. You'll get nothing in there except odd looks.

Arthur Not looking for anything.

The girls are miming a discussion at the back of the stage.

Frontier Guard I'm not supposed to allow jeans, for a start.

Arthur For old times' sake, mate.

*The **Porter** appears behind the two girls. He throws a shape and grins.*

Porter Howya girls?

Girls (*together*) Fuck off.

*They approach the door again and queue behind **Arthur.***

Frontier Guard (*points*) And the sweat-shirt, not allowed. A strict rule that, you need a shirt to get in here now.

Arthur *looks behind at the girls.*

Arthur So if I had a shirt . . . any shirt?

Frontier Guard They'd be no problem.

Arthur (*turning to the **Friend***) Hey, do us a favour. Lend us your blouse for a moment.

Friend Shag off, will you. (*Calls.*) Frank?

Arthur (*to girl*) How about you? I'll give it back to you inside.

Kathy What would I wear?

Arthur Straight swap. (*He grins.*) Come on. Chance it.

*He removes his jacket and peels off his T-shirt to stand bare-chested before her. He holds out the T-shirt to her. **Kathy** looks at her friend and then back at him before she unbuttons her blouse and hands it to him.*

Arthur Thanks. (*He puts it on with difficulty and buttons it up. Turns.*) Bit tight, but it will do. (*To the **Frontier***

Guard.) Well . . . any other objections?

Frontier Guard   What the. . . ? Don't get fresh with me, pal, right. I work out every day.

Arthur   Weights?

Frontier Guard   Weights, press-ups, sprints, you name it. So watch yourself.

Arthur   Can you. . . ? Naw, it's a bit hard.

Frontier Guard   Do what? I can do it.

Arthur   Naw, it's . . . tough.

Frontier Guard   Don't get fresh. Two hours a day. I can do it.

Arthur   Okay then, you've got to spread your legs really really wide, then lean forward as far as you can with just one hand on the ground supporting all your weight. You need to be super-fit, mind you.

Frontier Guard   Bullshit, I'll show you.

He spreads his legs and throws himself forward, balancing on one hand. **Kathy** *watches, teetering on laughter as the* **Friend** *hushes her.*

Arthur   But put your hand really out far, spread yourself!

The **Frontier Guard** *is almost spread-eagle on the stage now. The* **Porter** *drunkenly approaches, looks at him in astonishment, then slips through the doorway behind his back.* **Arthur** *goes to follow.*

Arthur   Now put your other hand right up in the air and wave!

As the **Frontier Guard** *does so* **Kathy** *is unable to contain her laughter. He suddenly realises how totally ridiculous he looks and snaps back to his feet.*

Frontier Guard (*realising* **Arthur** *is gone*)   The cheeky

bastard. He won't get out so easy. Wait till Tommy
comes on. We'll sort him. (*Turns to girls.*) What do you
want now?

Friend   Frank. She didn't mean it . . . what she said.
Can we get in?

Frontier Guard (*nods his head towards door*)   Go on.

The **Friend** *slips past him and as* **Kathy** *is about to follow,*
Frontier Guard *puts his hand out to block her.*

Frontier Guard (*to the* **Friend**)   Go on. I just want a
few words with your friend here in the silly jacket.

Kathy   Sharon, don't. Wait.

Frontier Guard   Go on, she'll be in in a minute. Go
on now or I'll bar you.

The **Friend** *vanishes.* **Frontier Guard** *turns to* **Kathy**.

Frontier Guard   Think you're smart, do you?
Anything else you want to take off? Don't let me stop
you.

Kathy   No, I'm . . . (*Almost a whisper.*) sorry.

Frontier Guard   What did you say?

Kathy (*quietly*)   I said, I'm sorry.

Frontier Guard   Can't hear you?

Kathy   I'm sorry for what I said.

Frontier Guard   You be nice to Frank and Frank will
be nice to you. (*Puts his arm around her as she tries to wriggle
free.*) One kiss for Frank, show that we're pals.

Kathy   Listen, I have to join my friend.

Frontier Guard   She'll wait. Just one. On the cheek,
go on. (*Holds her firmer.*)

Kathy   Please.

Frontier Guard   One.

*She reluctantly kisses him slightly on the cheek and shivers. She
darts from his arms and tries to avoid his hand slapping against
her as she slips past.*

Frontier Guard   All the same you girls. See you on
the way out, love.

As she passes the music soars up. The **Frontier Guard** *lifts
the platform away to one side.* **Arthur** *and the* **Friend** *come
forward.* **Arthur** *has the blouse in his hand.*

Friend (*sharply*)   Go on, give it back to her.

Arthur *throws her blouse across to her.*

Friend   Give him his thing. God knows what germs . . .

Kathy *takes off his T-shirt, hesitates, then throws it across to*
Arthur. *They look at each other before the* **Friend** *pulls her
away.*

Friend (*whispering*)   Jesus, you almost blew it again. I'm
sick of getting you out of scraps.

Kathy   But he . . .

Friend   Leave him for Tommy and Frank.

They are caught up in the sweep of music as the **Porter** *and the*
Frontier Guard *bounce forward, dancing. The girls join them,
swaying back and forth. Music dips slightly as girls stop and
confer briefly.*

Kathy   What's your one like?

Friend   Big-headed. You know what they say, big
head, small . . .

*She gestures downward and they laugh, starting to sway to louder
music.* **Arthur** *re-emerges to stare around him. He sees* **Kathy**
and walks towards her, tapping her shoulder. **Kathy** *turns in a
defensive stance. Her* **Friend** *looks over her shoulder at her.
Music dips again.*

Kathy What do you want?

Arthur Just to dance.

Kathy Why?

Arthur I didn't know you needed a reason when I used to dance here.

Kathy You do now. They're going to get you, you know. Frank's just waiting for his mate to come in.

Arthur I'll be gone before then. Only wanted a look around. I used to dance here once. Come on, one dance.

Kathy (*doubtful*) One dance?

She nods and they begin to dance. She tries to size him up as they move.

You're old for in here . . . are you married?

He laughs and shakes his head.

If me mate sees me with you again she'll think I'm after your pension.

Arthur Who gives a toss what people think?

They continue dancing for a moment.

Kathy You dance well for an old fellow.

Arthur The Black-and-Tans taught us the steps when I was young.

She laughs as they move together, drawn into the dance.

Kathy You were funny . . . with Frank.

Arthur I saw an old Turk do it to a German foreman. The whole factory stopped work, everybody cracking up. Eventually the foreman joined in as well . . . then they split the old Turk's head open.

As the music stops they are left cold, paralysed for a moment. Her

Friend *calls over to her.*

Friend   Kathy!

Kathy *looks back at her* **Friend**, *suddenly embarrassed.*

Friend   Are you coming or what? (*She stares at* **Arthur**, *protective of* **Kathy**.) Come on, will you!

Kathy *suddenly shrugs* **Arthur**'s *hand from her shoulder.*

Kathy (*low voice to* **Arthur**)   No, it's crazy.

Arthur   What?

Kathy   Find somebody your own age.

Arthur   Age isn't important. Only for horses and greyhounds. Listen . . .

Kathy (*confused*)   Please. Can't you see? It is for me!

Arthur (*stepping back*)   I'm sorry. I didn't . . . I'm sorry.

She turns to walk back to her **Friend** *as the music resumes and* **Arthur** *backs away from her, deflated, moving tiredly away towards the back of the stage. The music suddenly stops and all the cast (except* **Arthur***) turn as one to rush towards the front of the stage, shouting together.*

Cast   Taxi!

Arthur *joins the queue as their voices jumble together:*

Porter   No, he's not getting sick, he always walks like that.

Frontier Guard   I was here first, mate. Shove over there.

Friend   Please, Clondalkin, there's two of us.

Kathy (*back at* **Frontier Guard**)   Quit pushing, will you?

Porter   Just up to . . . shag it.

Their heads move as one, watching the taxi move away without them. **Kathy** *sees* **Arthur** *who glances at her before walking away.*

Friend (*joking*)   You need a minder. Bleeding geriatric he was. Are you trying to get us a bad name? I mean I know he qualifies for free travel and all, but . . .

Kathy   Just leave him alone, will you.

Friend   Well, at least you could have brought him home to meet your da unlike those two punks we met last week. Himself and your da could have had a great time reminiscing about the Emergency and rationing . . .

Kathy   Give over, Sharon. He beat the creep you were dancing with.

Friend   At least my fellow had his own teeth.

Kathy   Sharon, you make everything so . . .

Friend   I'd love a burger.

The cast (except **Arthur***) fall again into a queue in a burger shop, voices calling over each other.*

Porter   Double Kentucky vomit burger with stale fries. I'm only messing, honest. Ah no, leave me alone.

Frontier Guard   I've been waiting here half the night.

Friend   Shift your hand or I'll burst you.

Kathy   I don't want a burger, Sharon.

Kathy *turns and glimpses* **Arthur** *at the back of the stage as he pulls his jacket tighter around himself, leaning on the wall of an imaginary quay. He shakes his head, as if trying to get his hearing back.*

Kathy   Sharon, there he is by the river. Just wait for me . . . a minute.

Friend   Don't be thick, Kathy, come on, will you.

Kathy   I just want to say goodbye to him.

Friend   There's Jimmy's parked outside the Savoy, he'll give us a lift. I'm going now.

Kathy (*as the* **Friend** *moves away*)   Sharon...

Hesitantly she approaches **Arthur**. *She pauses as he tries to clear his ears again, then taps him on the shoulder. She steps back as he turns.*

Kathy   You got out okay, I was worried...

Arthur   What, the bouncer? I called his bluff first time.

Kathy (*looking at him shaking his head*)   Are you...?

Arthur   The dance club. It's the hissing... like being underwater for a while when you come out.

Kathy   You mustn't be used to it.

Arthur   I'm not. It's been a long time since I was in there. And it was all live music then. I was there the night the police raided it when The Chosen Few were playing. I was only fourteen, but I was there. I saw Rory Gallagher with The Impact and Skid Row...

Kathy (*with increasing incomprehension*)   Who?

Arthur (*he looks at her*)   Just bands.

Kathy   Oh.

He looks out into the audience. She follows his gaze.

Kathy   The river, it's nice at night, disguised like.

Arthur   Do they still tell you at school, about O'Connell Street? The widest street in Europe, they used to say.

Kathy (*surprised*)   Don't know. (*Shrugs her shoulders.*) I never listened to them.

Arthur   'The widest street.' I used to believe them. That same old Turk said it to me once, about his village. But it's true of here too.

Kathy (*puzzled*)   What is?

Arthur   It's all smaller, different when you return.
Look at it . . . O'Connell Street. Just like some honky-
tonk provincial plaza. Everywhere closed except the
burger huts, all the buses gone, everyone milling around
drunk, taking to the glittering lights like aborigines to
whiskey. Just like some provincial kip I've seen dozens
of. (*Pauses.*) But it all seemed so grand once. As a kid I
remember . . . being choked up, staring down at it, as
far as the eye could see . . . as a treat from the Pillar.

Kathy   The what?

Arthur   Nelson's.

Kathy (*laughs*)   Jesus, I wasn't born when that was
blown up. (*Suddenly embarrassed.*) Sorry, it must make you
feel . . .

Arthur (*quietly*)   No, I deserve it. I'm talking too much.

Kathy   I keep doing that, don't I?

Arthur   No, you're right.

Kathy (*hesitantly*)   I didn't mean to hurt you.

Arthur   Go on back. You'll meet somebody.

Kathy   No. I've had enough. I hate it. My friend's
annoyed with me anyway, she's gone on.

Arthur   How will you get home?

Kathy   I'll get a taxi. I have the money.

Arthur   I'll take you home if you let me.

Kathy *looks at him uncertainly.*

Kathy   Have you a car?

He grins and shakes his head as they begin to walk.

Arthur   No, we're out of miracles – there was a run of
them earlier. I've a motorbike, bought it when I came

home. It broke me, but shag it. Couldn't afford one when I was growing up. Always swore I'd get one, roar down all the lanes I knew as a kid. It's stupid I suppose. Bread and margarine till I get work, but you'd get a pain in your hole being sensible. Do you want to risk it?

Kathy   I survived the dancing clones. I'd say I'll survive it. It has an engine at least?

Arthur   This thing would take you across the Sahara desert.

Kathy   Will it get us to Clondalkin?

Arthur   Jaysus, I'd sooner chance the Sahara desert, but we'll give it a lash. Here, mind your man.

The **Porter** *is leaning on the barrel. He sways forward, singing, then leans on it again for support and looks at them.*

Porter   Giz a cigarette, go on, will you?

Arthur   Sorry mate, I haven't any.

Porter   Go on, giz . . .

The **Porter** *sinks his head down as* **Arthur** *leads* **Kathy** *over towards a motor-bike helmet at the side of the stage. The* **Frontier Guard** *and* **Friend** *emerge, playing a married couple.*

Frontier Guard   It ruined the play, darling. There was no need to say that at the interval, just because he was wearing jeans at the theatre.

Friend   All I asked him was why wasn't he out minding the cars.

Frontier Guard (*producing car keys*)   He was a member of the audience, love. He was just wearing jeans.

Friend   Well he looked like the lad in the cap you gave the money to.

Frontier Guard   Oh, my God!

He crosses the stage, searching, then turns to dart back the way he has come. The **Friend** *follows him, as the* **Porter** *lifts himself away from the barrel.*

Arthur   The bike is here by the monument.

Porter   Is the last 19 gone?

Arthur   Gone, mate, gone. It's after twelve.

Porter   The last 22?

Arthur   They're all gone.

Porter   The 16s or the 3s?

Arthur (*straightening*)   All the buses are in bed. It's safe to cross the road.

The **Porter** *sways across the stage, catching hold of the raised platform which almost falls on his head.* **Arthur** *takes it from him and lays it on its side.*

Frontier Guard   Oh, my God, darling!

Friend   What?

Frontier Guard   The Volvo? Our new Volvo is gone!

Friend   Oh, darling!

Frontier Guard (*to* **Arthur**)   You there, excuse me. My new Volvo, gone. It was there, did you see. . . ?

Arthur   No, I'm sorry mate. I'm just after coming along.

Porter (*to* **Arthur**)   What's wrong with him? What's up?

Arthur (*bending down for the helmet*)   His flash Volvo. It's gone.

Porter (*approaching the* **Frontier Guard**)   Your last Rolo? It's gone. Here, I'll give you a hand looking.

He looks around while the **Frontier Guard** *and the* **Friend** *stand back in horror from him. They walk off and the* **Porter** *follows.*

Porter   Here, I'll take a lift off you.

Arthur *hands* **Kathy** *the helmet.*

Kathy   Have you only one helmet? What about you?

Arthur   Take it.

Kathy *takes it and raises it over her head as her recorded voice begins to speak. They stand for a moment as if astride a bike and the lights move to suggest speed with slots of white as they pass beneath lamp-posts.*

Kathy's voice
  I accepted it like a pledge
  And my arms circled your leather jacket
  Your hair blown into my face
  We raced up the quays towards my estate

  Down a lane choked with scrap
  Among the rust-eaten ghosts of lorries
  Within sight of my father's house
  Is where I first loved Arthur Cleary

The engine dies with the last line of the poem. **Kathy** *mimes getting off a bike and turns to face* **Arthur**. *He goes to help her remove the helmet but she steps back, defining her territory. She takes the helmet off, waits a moment, then tosses it over to him. She fixes her hair and looks at him. They are both silent, in their private thoughts.* **Arthur** *leans on the edge of the platform.*

Arthur   That dance club. I was stupid to go back. That used to be my regular. It was crazy to think the same people might be there, but they all seem to have vanished. It was one of the few places I knew that's still standing. I suppose they're all married by now. Mortgages, ulcers, overdrafts. Far from dancing on their minds.

Kathy   Where were you?

Arthur   Places . . . all much the same, you forget the names.

Kathy   Glad to be back?

Arthur   Just got to get my bearings. You know, it feels like only months I was away and yet you keep turning corners and what should be there isn't there. Sorry, I really am talking too much.

Kathy   No.

Arthur   A great place to talk, that's how I remember it. Meeting people, hours passing, evenings, winding up in rooms still talking. Funny – say hello to people now they look at you. Think it's all I've said in the last week – ten fags, milk, the paper, '*Zwei Brötchen und einige Käse*' – they look at you like you've ten heads – oh Jaysus, sorry, a scabby sliced pan please.

Kathy   You're funny.

Arthur   How do you mean?

Kathy   Don't know . . . different. (*Pause.*) Why'd you come back to this kip?

Arthur   I belong in this kip. It's like at the end of a night, you know, you have to go home.

Kathy   You're welcome to it. If I had a chance I would be gone tomorrow. Anywhere – just out of here. Somewhere anonymous, the freedom of some city where if you walked down the longest street not one person would care who you are or where you're from.

Arthur   That can be lonely too.

Kathy   You can live with loneliness. You can't live here. (*She climbs awkwardly onto the top of the barrel and looks at him.*) You're different somehow, you're still breathing. Maybe because you got out. Sometimes . . . don't laugh . . . sometimes I think they've sucked all the air out of this city and people are walking around opening and closing their mouths with nothing coming in, nothing going out. (*She blushes and laughs, jumping down in embarrassment.*) And that sounds crazy, I know.

Arthur   No. Some nights working in a canning factory in Denmark I'd stand up on the loading bay beside the hoist and I'd look down at three in the morning on the workers below, nobody speaking, the limbs moving automatically, the curious stillness behind all the bustle. And I'd start thinking it was the conveyor belt and the loading machine that were alive, that they were thinking 'more cans for the arms', and at seven in the morning the machines would stop and the arms of the men would move back and forth till somebody remembered to press a switch. So maybe I'm crazy too, but that's why I came home.

Kathy *approaches him. She lifts her arms, then folds them awkwardly behind her back. He does the same.*

Arthur (*hesitantly*)   How old?

Kathy   Eighteen. (*Pause.*) And you?

Arthur (*beat*)   Thirty-five.

She walks behind the platform in embarrassment and leans on it, playing for time to think.

Kathy (*softly*)   You don't think I'm a slut?

He smiles and shakes his head.

Kathy   You're not gay, are you?

He laughs.

Arthur   No. (*Laughs again.*) Why do you ask?

Kathy   Don't know. I suppose ... well, you haven't tried anything. (*Quickly.*) Not that I want you to, like ... but often lads can be pushy, just want to get you out by yourself and then get away.

Arthur   So did I once. So did everyman.

Kathy *comes back around to face him.*

Kathy   You won't take the wrong idea about me?

Arthur   I'll only take whatever idea you want.

Kathy   Will you. . . ?

They embrace and kiss. There is an interplay of light to suggest time passing. **Kathy** *turns so that she is still in* **Arthur**'s *arms but facing away from him. They are silent, in their private thoughts.*

Arthur   It was the strangest thing.

Kathy (*looks up*)   What?

Arthur   The church. Near the flats. There was such an overspill of people living there that they put up a temporary one. The tin one they called it – a sort of huge prefab. Inside as a child you'd hear the rain splattering against the corrugated tin roof. I'd forgotten that sound till one winter in a Dutch factory . . . sleeping in those long iron dormitories, the Turks, the Moluccans, the first few of the Irish. I'd wake at night and remember . . . like it would always be there, a part of me . . . to return to. (*Stops.*) The first night I got home I went walking, past buildings boarded up, new names over shops. I came to the lane where the church had been. There was a crackling sound, then I smelt the smoke. They were clearing the site for apartments. There were just the girders of the church left and everything else still smouldering, waiting to be shifted. Hadn't been there or in any other church since I was fifteen. But it was in my mind as something to come home to that would never change.

Listening to him, **Kathy** *suddenly shivers and steps away.*

Arthur (*concerned*)   What's wrong?

Kathy (*retreating behind the barrel*)   I don't know. You know that feeling like this has happened before.

Suddenly . . . it scared me.

Arthur   Shush . . . it will be dawn soon. Did you ever wait up for the dawn?

Kathy *shakes her head.*

Arthur (*approaching her*)   So strange, you're exhausted, you can't go on, and then . . . I felt it on so many nights working in factories . . . the first hint of light and you can feel it through your body, energy, from nowhere, strength you didn't know you had from deep within you . . . Then the dawn comes and it floods you. Hey . . .

Kathy   What?

Arthur   Never thought I'd . . . feel new again, like now . . .

Kathy (*moving away, this time behind the platform which she leans on*)   Arthur, I don't want to hear . . . you scare me, I don't always understand you . . . you don't talk like real people.

Arthur   Real people?

Silently the **Porter** *and the* **Friend** *emerge on stage. The* **Porter** *stands at the front left while the* **Friend** *who has donned a mask stands with her back to the audience.*

Kathy   You know what I mean . . . safe. (*She points.*) See that house, with the light still on.

Arthur (*looking*)   Yeah.

Kathy   That's his light, it will burn till I go in. Never this late before. He'll be worried . . . listening for me. It's funny . . . when I was young and he was working he talked like you . . . like he wasn't scared of looking over his shoulder . . . like . . .

The **Porter** *suddenly turns, his face white with anger, his hands clenched.* **Arthur** *retreats from* **Kathy**.

Porter   And now you're taking up with this fellow, this knacker.

Kathy   He's not, Dad.

Porter   Well, whatever he is, he's too old for you. Can't you see child? He's no job, he's got nothing. Good Christ, I worked hard enough all these years to try and get you something, to try and lift you up. Where's he going, where can he bring you? Some corporation flat. You're only a child yet. You're throwing your life away for him.

Kathy   It's not serious Dad, I've only met him twice. I'm not even sure about him. It's just that he's . . . different. There's something . . .

Porter   Different! May be different to you but I've seen his like all my life. Every week they'd be another one of them in the factory and within the month they'd be gone. Fly-boys. Drifters. Only certainty was that they'd be gone. How could he build a life for you like I've tried to build for your mother? Tell me that? A knacker in a leather jacket, with one hand longer than the other and the rattle of his bike waking the street at every hour of the night. What's so special about him then?

Kathy   He's not dead! He's not beaten! He's . . .

Porter (*quietly*)   Like I am, is it? Beaten?

There is a pause while the mood changes. Then **Kathy** *speaks quietly.*

Kathy   Do you remember, Dad? Bull Island? (**Porter** *smiles ruefully.*) The thrill of hiding up there in the sand-dunes waiting for you to find me, peering out at you climbing up. Remember?

Porter   I'd park the car on the strand and you'd be gone before my back was turned. Always running. A proper little rascal.

Kathy *runs across the stage with childish strides to hide behind the barrel as he comes looking for her. She runs out, avoiding him, then looks over her shoulder for a moment with hands clenched, giggling. He circles and when she tries to run he catches her and throws her up in his arms. She shouts for him to let go and as he lowers her down she puts her feet on his shoes so that she is dancing with him like a child with her father. A note of sadness enters his voice.*

Porter   That was a good car that. I kept it well.

Kathy   You'll have a car again Dad. Only a matter of time.

The **Porter** *lets her go, looking down at his hands in a gesture of futility.*

Kathy   You looked after us well Dad. You still do.

Porter   Feel so useless, love. I wish I was dead sometimes. You'd have the insurance then at least.

Kathy (*as she runs to him*)   Daddy, don't say that. Don't wish it. You're the best.

Porter (*pulling the platform back up and pushing it into place fiercely as he speaks*)   I've good hands. I can make things with these. Give me wood and I'll make it. Tables, chairs, shelves. I never thought I'd be idle with these. A skill for life they said. Always find something.

Kathy   It doesn't matter, Daddy. You've done so much, all your life. It's time to rest now.

Porter   The women cried the day we left. Out in the open at the gates of the factory. The television were there. All the fuss, the papers. Then they left us alone. With just our thoughts.

Lights fade on him and **Kathy** *and switch to* **Arthur** *standing beside the barrel and to the* **Friend** *who turns with a white mask over her face.*

Arthur   Ma. I know you can't hear, but I talk to you still. You have to talk to someone.

Friend   I know, son. I talked to you often enough those years you were abroad.

Arthur   I was never one for writing, Ma.

Friend   Never expected you to, son. You had your own life.

Arthur   She's so much younger than me, Ma. All the lads I knew, they're all gone. Girls with prams, so suddenly old.

Friend (*softly*)   Fifteen years son. A sorrowful decade and a half.

Arthur   We had our joyful one.

Friend (*ironic as she slowly lowers the mask*)   How often did I see you on your knees telling your rosary beads?

Arthur (*laughs*)   As often as I saw you.

Friend   Still, we had our good times.

Arthur   Mornings I'd climb down the steps from these flats and people would shout, 'Arthur Cleary! Arthur Cleary! Come in! Come in!'

Friend   Me laughing from the balcony at your mates trying to dance like Zorba the Greek!

Arthur   Closing time Fridays walking up from town, playing football in the traffic. Remember I'd bring you a Baby Power and we'd sit round drinking bottles of Guinness from brown paper bags.

Friend   At three in the morning, they'd still be arriving. 'Is that Arthur Cleary's? Have we found the place?'

Arthur   This is the place, but now I can't find them. Ma, I can't find you. I can't find my old self. Feel so old . . . except when she's beside me. (*He looks down, then* *up again.*) Mrs Burke told me, Ma, how you lived out those last years on white bread and tea.

Friend   They barred me from the pub son, when the new owners did it up. Barred when I was the first woman who refused to be corralled inside the snug years before. Singing they said I was. What's a pub for only singing?

Arthur   You broke your hip trying to cross the road when a security van broke the lights.

Friend   Shagging Culchie drivers.

Arthur   I wasn't running from you, Ma. You know that, don't you? (*She doesn't answer.*) It was just . . . the time. So easy to drift between jobs and places, it just seemed right to wander off for a while and then wander back. Only I never did. Oh, I often imagined it, arriving back with no warning or nothing, just turning up at dawn with a bottle of brandy and the stubble of three days' travel. (*Quietly.*) Only it wasn't like that, was it?

Friend   You've never been to the grave, son. Though I was never there myself before I went to keep him company in it.

Arthur   Had a drink for you Ma instead. Knew you'd prefer that. Among the disco lights and the canned music. And sang 'Who Fears to Speak of Easter Week' for you. The owner almost shat himself. I think he thought I was cracked.

Friend   When did we ever give a shite what any of them thought of us, son?

Arthur   When did we ever, Ma? (*Pause.*) Why am I talking to you, Ma? The dead cannot talk.

Friend   They can, son. But only among themselves.

Lights fade on the **Friend** *on the final word as* **Arthur** *looks at her, suddenly frightened. Lights rise on* **Kathy** *holding the* *motor-bike helmet in her hands.* **Arthur** *approaches her cautiously. She looks at him, then silently hands him the helmet back. He looks down at it, then walks slowly to the edge of the stage where he puts it down.* **Kathy** *backs away, then silently approaches the* **Porter** *and mimes saying goodbye. Her hand rests for a moment on his shoulder, her lips lightly touching the back of his neck. The* **Friend** *crosses the stage and* **Kathy** *approaches her.*

Friend   Did you say goodbye to him, like we agreed?

Kathy   I did. He was waiting for me along the quays, staring at the water as usual. I didn't think I'd have the courage. 'Arthur, I'm sorry,' I said ... 'it's just too big an age gap, it's not right.' He never spoke, Sharon, his face looked old, suddenly, like all the air had drained from it.

Friend   I know it's hard, you were fairly gone on him but it's for the best. You'll see. It will be like old times again.

Kathy   All the way home, felt like throwing myself from the bus. I came in, Sharon, saw my father, just sitting, staring at the television. And I remembered a man who feared no other, a brown wage packet left on an oilskin table. If he could only cry, I could stay with him, but his kind were never taught how to show grief. I need to learn to breathe. Sharon, I need Arthur and I don't know how to ask him, to teach me ... to wake up and not be afraid of what the day will bring. (*Pause.*) I've packed a bag, Sharon. If he'll take me in I'll go to him, or I'll go somewhere else, anywhere, but I don't fit here any more. (*Pause.*) Will you be glad for me?

Friend   What's wrong with here?

Kathy   You hate it, you always say you do.

Friend   But I'll settle for it. I'm not running half-cocked after anybody. Real life isn't like that. This isn't a bleeding movie Kathy, real people don't do this.

You're even starting to talk like that header.

Kathy   I can't breathe here, Sharon.

Friend   Have you ever tried opening and closing your mouth? For God's sake, Kathy, your man's a fossil and he doesn't need to breathe. You're just walking out, leaving me.

Kathy   Not you, I'll see you the same, just . . .

Friend   How could it be the same . . . you, me and him? Been calling for you since I was five . . . for school, dances, mitching out, covering up for you. And you say it will be the same. We were never good enough for you, isn't that right?

Kathy   Sharon, please.

Friend   You'll beg for one of these houses one day. You'll settle for a squalling brat and Yellow Pack bread and a thrill off the fridge, if you're lucky. Just like the rest of us.

Kathy   I'm going, Sharon.

Friend   Go on then and good luck, kid. 'Cause I won't know you when you're running back in a week's time with your tail between your legs. Do you hear?

The **Friend** *storms off stage and* **Kathy** *is left alone as the* **Porter** *walks silently away. Her recorded voice is heard.*

Kathy's voice
I had a room with fresh linen
And parents to watch over me
A brown dog slept at my feet
I left them for Arthur Cleary.

The lights change to suggest dawn. **Arthur** *is still standing at the edge of stage. He now moves forward holding a bunch of keys in his hand.* **Kathy** *approaches and stands a few feet away, as he stops, surprised to see her.*

Kathy Been walking all night, round and round these flats. (*Pause.*) I left them Arthur. Am I crazy or what?

Arthur I don't know. And I don't care, except you're here.

*He throws her the keys and they embrace. Lights go down and the sinister music from the first **Frontier Guard** scene returns. When a weak light returns it shines above **Arthur**'s head as he stands alone against the wooden platform with the **Porter** shining his torch up and down the bars from behind. The **Frontier Guard** approaches and shines a second torch at **Arthur**'s face.*

Frontier Guard Passport please.

Arthur *recovers.*

Arthur Oh, sorry.

*He hands him a passport which the **Frontier Guard** examines.*

Frontier Guard Ah Irish. Irish. Boom-boom! eh! (*He laughs.*)

Arthur Yeah. Boom-bleeding-boom.

*The **Frontier Guard** hands him back the passport.*

Arthur Eh? Where am I now? Which side of the border am I on?

Frontier Guard What does it matter to you, Irish? Either side you are a long way from home.

Arthur (*shrugs his head towards the light behind him*) What's he looking at the wheels for?

Frontier Guard Looking for? (*Laughs.*) It is the rules, Irish. We will go on soon. (*He turns to leave him.*)

Arthur (*suddenly puzzled*) Wait, have you . . . eh, have you checked my passport before?

Frontier Guard *returns, shining his torch into **Arthur**'s eyes.*

Frontier Guard   Before? Only once we check.

Arthur   Well then, do I know you from somewhere?

Frontier Guard   Maybe you take this train before, Irish?

Arthur   No, somewhere else. Somewhere different.

Frontier Guard   You know a brothel called BB's in Stuttgart?

Arthur   No.

Frontier Guard   Neither do I! (*He laughs heartily.*) Funny, eh?

Arthur   I do know you. Wait.

He looks closely at the man who shrugs his shoulders and walks away behind the platform. Suddenly the **Porter** *and the* **Frontier Guard** *begin to sing in a Dublin accent.*

Frontier Guard *and* **Porter**   Ah poor old Dicey Riley she has taken to the sup, sup, sup!

Frontier Guard *comes back round and stares at* **Arthur**. *He holds his hand out and speaks in his 'Deignan' voice.*

Frontier Guard   Hey, wait a minute. (*He shakes his hand.*) I know you.

Reverting back to the **Frontier Guard** *he walks back behind platform, leaving* **Arthur** *confused and frightened.*

Frontier Guard *and* **Porter** (*singing as they exit*)
Poor oul Dicey Riley, she will never give it up!

Lights hit blackout and return to the noise of a bang. We see the **Porter** *scampering, with child-like steps, across the stage to exit at far side. The* **Frontier Guard** *emerges with a leather-bound book in his hand and shouts.*

Frontier Guard (*in a whinging money-lender's voice*)
Frankie! Young Frankie Doyle! I saw you there,
I'm no fool, you know. Come back here, tell your

mother I want to see her.

Arthur *stands with his arms around* **Kathy** *beside the platform. The* **Friend** *emerges on the right side of stage.*

Frontier Guard (*politely to the* **Friend** *as he turns*)   Ah, Mrs Burke. Fine weather.

Friend   The better for not being in your clutches, Mr Deignan.

Frontier Guard   Always here to help, Mrs Burke.

Friend   Go and shite.

She exits.

Frontier Guard (*smiles after her*)   Charming. (*He turns back to an imaginary door and shouts.*) I know you're in there, Mrs Doyle! I'm not a fool, you know. If you can't pay them you shouldn't take out loans. (*He consults his ledger.*) Mrs Doyle, didn't I see young Frankie from the car driving up the flats. Three weeks Mrs Doyle, three weeks. God would have made the world three times. You'd think that husband of yours could have made three pounds even. Easy knowing the creator of heaven and earth didn't come from this block of flats.

Suddenly the **Frontier Guard** *sees* **Arthur** *and* **Kathy**.

Frontier Guard   Eh, what are you at then? (**Arthur** *and* **Kathy** *ignore him.*) Head-the-ball, I'm talking to you!

Arthur (*quietly*)   I live here.

Frontier Guard   Since when? Old Mrs Cleary used to live there.

Arthur   I was born here.

Frontier Guard   Tell me another. I've had me eye on that place since the oul bat died. A troublesome oul biddy she was too. This law and that law. (*He snorts.*)

Arthur (*quietly*)   Nice to know my mother had such a

concerned friend.

Frontier Guard (*snaps fingers*)   Wait a minute. I have you. Arthur! Arthur Cleary! Sure, wasn't I a year behind you in school. Deignan, Larry Deignan. My mother had the shop on the corner. Sure, I used to look up to you. Only the mother, you know, wasn't too keen on you. (*Pause.*) So, the famous son eh, the wanderer.

Arthur   Will you stop.

The **Frontier Guard** *approaches.*

Frontier Guard   No offence meant Arthur. I thought you were just squatters. (*He puts out hand.*) You get some dodgy types around here.

Arthur (*ignoring hand*)   So I see.

Frontier Guard   Don't know what brought you back. Great to see you all the same. Do you remember . . . the day you had to be dug out of old McCarthy, the teacher, the day you were expelled from school? God, you were a legend then. You remember me, Arthur? Don't you? And the mother? The little shop on the corner. Here, I'll give you my card. I could be of use to you settling in.

Arthur   I remember the firelighter.

Frontier Guard (*bewildered*)   The what?

Arthur   The young tinker lad my mother gave a threepenny bit to once. He went looking for sweets in your mother's shop. She gave him a firelighter and a penny change. He thought it was coconut and stuffed it in his mouth. You must remember him now, you were laughing about it long enough. Never able to speak again. I used to see him begging near the Four Courts. Your mother always said, it will teach his sort a lesson. (*He gives a slight laugh.*) Yeah, I remember her well.

Frontier Guard *moves closer as if about to strike* **Arthur**, *then gives a little laugh.*

Frontier Guard   Always the jokes, Arthur, eh. I'll leave you my card. It will be a pleasure hearing from you.

*He presses it into **Arthur**'s hand and exits. **Arthur** looks at it, then tears it up and exits into where the flat would be. **Kathy** who has been leaning on the platform during this now comes forward and carefully picks up the pieces of the card to stare at them before exiting with them held in her hand.*

Act Two

A motorbike engine is heard for a moment in blackout before it is switched off and the soundtrack takes on a rural feel as lights come up. There is a shout before **Arthur** *enters at a trot as though after coming down a slope and turns to catch* **Kathy** *who rushes on after him.*

Arthur No problem to you. I told you so.

Kathy No problem for you in those boots. The feet are stung off me. There's nettles up there like bamboos.

Arthur We'll soon be rid of those. (*He kneels to pluck imaginary leaves from ground and rub them into her legs.*) Dock leaves. Your only men. (**Kathy** *looks around her.*) Well, was I right? Knocksedan. Isn't it great?

Kathy Tell me about it again.

He stops rubbing and looks up at her.

Arthur Sure, can't you see it with your own eyes?

Kathy It's not the same. It's only weeds and bushes and rocks, but when you describe it it's special, it's your world.

Arthur (*looking around him*) It's as much yours as mine. That's what's special about it . . . it's just here, it's anybody's.

Kathy It's not here, Arthur. Not the way you knew it. With other people . . . well places seem to pass before them like scenes in a film, but with you it's all kept inside – everywhere's special.

Arthur It's just a place.

Kathy All you have are places . . . and the dole.

Arthur We manage.

Kathy (*going to sit on the barrel*) You're a sap, Arthur

Cleary and I'm worse for going along with you. Tell me about this place. Come on. Who did you come here with?

Arthur *comes over for her to climb on his shoulders. They stand staring out at the audience.*

Arthur Anyone who would come. Or just alone.

Kathy Girls?

Arthur Girls who'd go sick from the factories to swim here in the river with me. Two hours persuading them to take their dresses off for five minutes in the water. (*Grins.*) But it was worth it. That mound there. (*He points.*) It's man-made. Older than Christ. Some evenings I'd climb up there in the dusk and it was as though you could almost hear it saying to you: 'I know you. I know everything you will ever feel. I have felt it all before.'

Kathy More likely it was saying: 'Stop standing on my skull, you're giving me a headache.' Hills don't talk, Arthur. (*She looks around her again.*) Was this always here?

Arthur Of course.

Kathy Never saw it or knew it. All these hidden bits of the city ... like a film set that I swear wasn't here yesterday. (*Her voice changes.*) Six weeks today, Arthur.

Arthur You should go back, see him.

Kathy Tell him what ... now I know Knocksedan and The Pigeon House and Howth Head at night and the lanes off Thomas Street. Jesus, Arthur, you couldn't explain that to real people ... it's not real life, that's what Sharon said.

Arthur What's real life – a clean job, pretending you own some mortgaged house on an estate, death from cancer at forty?

Kathy That's what Sharon said I'd settle for. This is so good it frightens me ... (*She taps his skull as though it* *was wooden.*) Arthur, are you listening to me?

Arthur   I am in my granny. I'm wondering are the logs still down there that you could cross the river by. We'll climb down and have a gander.

Kathy   Jesus, more nettles, more briars.

Arthur *lowers her down along his back.*

Arthur   Sure a little prick won't do you any harm.

Kathy   Oh, are you coming as well, so?

She runs away as he chases after her in mock anger to the edge of the platform which she mounts. Picking up his helmet, she places it on his head back-to-front. She turns him round, then with a little kick spins him out into the middle of the stage.

Sinister music begins as she retreats and both the **Frontier Guard** *and the* **Porter** *emerge.* **Arthur** *gropes his way forward until his foot hits against the box. He stops and takes his helmet off. The* **Frontier Guard** *and the* **Porter** *have formed themselves into a queue behind him, slouching with the look of broken men.* **Arthur** *is standing facing the barrel, staring around as if confused as to how he got there. The imaginary queue in front of him moves in a sequence of short mimed jerks, during which* **Arthur** *glances behind him past the* **Frontier Guard** *at the* **Porter**. *He turns away to move one step forward, then turns to look at the* **Porter** *again. During the ensuing conversation the crouching* **Frontier Guard** *keeps staring belligerently between them.*

Arthur   Johnny, isn't it? Johnny Carroll?

The **Porter** *looks suspicious, then recognises him.*

Porter   Arthur Cleary? I thought you were off in Germany?

Arthur   I was, but I'm back. (*Looks up.*) You'd have thought they would have painted the dole office in my absence. But, come here, I thought you were well in for life up there in McGuirks.

Porter I was. Till I was laid off. But that's four years ago. Sure that place is just a crater now. All that row of factories is the same. You can see them from the train with the roofs caved in. There's nothing here now, Arthur. Not like long ago.

Arthur Do you remember, where was it . . . that timber yard off Francis Street? We both started together at nine o'clock. A right hole. We left it at eleven. Told your man to fuck himself.

Porter And we were fixed up over in that carton factory in the Combe by lunchtime. Those were the days. There was always a start somewhere. Seems like another world now, being able to walk from one job to the next. If people get in anywhere these days they stick like glue.

Arthur Mind you, the carton factory was a hole too. What a weird bunch worked there. Remember what's his name (*Snaps his fingers.*) – Dockets?

Porter (*mock voice*) Have you a docket for that, son? Have you a docket? (*Normal voice.*) And the little guy in the white coat. You could hardly see his head over the machines.

Arthur We used to shout after him, (*Bends his knees to make himself smaller, hand over his mouth.*) 'Stop walking in that hole!' (*Looks around, indignantly.*) 'Who said that? If I catch the lad who said that he's fired.'

Porter Remember Boots?

Arthur Boots! For God's sake. I'd forgotten him. Refused to wear anything else, just the one pair day and night. We used to claim he slept in them.

Porter You had a song about him, remember? The Elvis voice, up on the pallet of cartons, doing all the movements with the brush. Remember Boots even caught you.

Arthur   How did it go?

Porter   Jaysus, it's a long time.

Arthur   Wait: (*Mock Elvis accent.*)
'My granny would like to roll and roll.'

He points at the **Porter** *waiting for a response.*

Porter
'But I'm too tired to dig her up.'

Together
'My goldfish would love a bowl
'Cause he hates crapping in a cup,
My wife's abandoned me,
But I don't care two hoots
'Cause all I really want to do
Is stomp around in black rubber wellington boots.'

*The two of them begin miming a dance during this to the
increasing bemusement of the* **Frontier Guard**. *Now with their
hands impersonating guitars they move in for the kill, getting closer
and closer together with each word until the* **Frontier Guard**
*is squashed between them, almost bent double with his hands still
in his pockets.*

Together
'Boots! Boots! Boots! Boots!'

Frontier Guard (*looking at* **Arthur**)   The King of
Rock'n'Roll, eh?

Porter   The real McCoy. Arthur Cleary.

Arthur   That's where we first met Eamonn,
remember –

Porter (*throws a shape*)   The original Rocker.

Arthur   Suede shoes, huge lapels on the jacket, the
whole works. Where's he now?

Porter (*quietly*)   He's fucking dead, Arthur. He blew his
own brains out last year. We're all fucking dead, Arthur,

or as good as, in this place.

Arthur   We've a few pints to sink before they lower us down yet. Do you remember the time . . . ?

Porter (*surly*)   No. It's gone.

Frontier Guard *nudges* **Arthur** *with his shoulder.*

Frontier Guard   Will you hurry fucking up. Some of us have to get back to work, you know.

Arthur (*studying the* **Frontier Guard**'s *face*)   Do I know you, mate?

Frontier Guard   You don't know nothing.

Arthur (*puzzled*)   From somewhere . . . that face. (*He moves forward to the barrel, then listens as if being addressed.*) Come back at half-two?

He steps back, deflated and picks up his helmet. The two men circle him.

Porter (*with a shrug*)   Welcome home, Arthur!

As they exit the **Friend** *enters, carrying a mask of a woman's face in each hand. The* **Friend** *speaks for both masks, changing her voice slightly for each. She moves the* **First Mask** *as if peering down from a balcony.*

First Mask   Come 'ere.

Second Mask   What?

First Mask   Come 'ere.

Second Mask   What?

Kathy *walks across the stage, miming turning a key in a lock and exits as the masks follow her movements.*

First Mask   That's her there, Phyllis! Moved in with him bold as brass and his mother barely cold in the grave. The young ones now. Would you be up to them? Never had that class of yoke here before he came back.

Second Mask   Wild like the mother, Mrs Doyle. And sure what harm are they doing? Isn't it good to see somebody smiling in this place?

First Mask   I don't know. A fool's paradise never lasts long. It's easy to smile without two children bawling, it's easy to smile when you don't have to sell your soul to that wee bastard every time an ESB bill comes in or one of them gets sick. (*Stops and stares off to left with alarm in her voice.*) Is that Mr Deignan's car, Phyllis, there stopped at the traffic lights?

Second Mask   No, that's just brown. His is shite coloured.

First Mask   Some days you'd be afraid to take the plug out of the sink in case his head would pop up. You know what Mrs Kennedy said to him: 'You're so famous round here Mr Deignan,' she said, 'They'll have you in the waxworks museum soon, only they won't need to make a model of you.'

Second Mask   Will you relax, Mrs Doyle, it's moving off. Lord, you're fierce jumpy. What you need now is a young toy boy.

First Mask   A toy boy? I'm lucky to get a bar of Kitkat and a lie in. Come 'ere to me. (*The masks are drawn closer and the voice drops.*) Do you know what he says to me the other morning, the youngest crying in the next room and him lying there with the teeth in the glass beside the bed? (*The* **Friend** *begins to lower the masks.*) He puts a hand out suddenly and says he, (*A gruff male mumble.*) 'Lie back Rosie, it's Saturday.'

Lights go down, then come up on **Arthur** *staring into space as if gazing from a window.* **Kathy** *is behind him, lying on the platform.*

Arthur   He's out there again.

Kathy   Who is?

Arthur Deignan.

Kathy Forget him.

Arthur (*bitterly*) God, I remember him now, a little
brat in short trousers, perpetual snot on his nose and
even then he could buy and sell you. He used to steal
sweets from the mother and flog them for half price.
Then when we were fourteen … I remember … it was
condoms, johnnies. Don't know where he got them, but
he told the whole school I'd bought four off him one
evening and came back the next day for two more.
Jaysus, they were buying them by the new-tide, every
penny they had … hidden under beds, going green,
never used … and back the next week for more in case
he'd tell people that they hadn't needed them.

Kathy *laughs.*

Arthur Before I went away I saw him one night out
in Monkstown … all the little rich kids with money and
no sense. He was selling them joints, ready-rolled for
half a crown. They were having to be carried home to
Mammy by their friends. I took a pull … herbal
tobacco and loose shag … he winked up at me, 'Do
you want a cut Arthur? Be my man here.' Christ, he
looked pathetic, the elephant flares, huge tie like a red
carpet. (*He pauses and his tone changes.*) I saw him yesterday
in Drumcondra. Collecting rent. He's four houses there
in flats. Warrens. You should have seen the number of
bells on every door.

Kathy Who gives a fuck about him? Come away,
Arthur.

Arthur That Doyle woman is with him. Like a dog
keeping its distance, terrified of a kick.

Kathy Arthur! You're like an old woman staring out
the window. You get on my nerves whenever he's
around.

Arthur *turns.*

Arthur   Have we tea?

Kathy   You know we haven't. We'll do without. It's not important.

Arthur   Dole day tomorrow.

Kathy   I know. It's okay.

Arthur   Bread?

Kathy   Arthur, stop this.

Arthur   It was easier by myself. I didn't mind the bad days. Just take to the bed, take them in my stride. But now . . .

Kathy   Don't, Arthur, please.

Arthur   You know I'm trying, love. Every old foreman I knew. Every factory that's left. I want to look after you.

Kathy *(screams)*   Stop! Can't you see? You'll become like them, you're sounding like my da. *(She rises as* **Arthur** *tries to speak.)* I'm not fragile. I'm not some ornament made of glass. I'm flesh and I'm blood. I don't need looking after – I need to live. Listen, you're different Arthur and I don't mind if we starve, just don't change, not for me.

Arthur   I just want to give you . . . things.

Kathy   I didn't come to you for things. I came to you for hope. I can do without anything, except that. Shag the tea and the bread, Arthur, just make me laugh.

He sits on the floor and looks up at her.

Arthur   The vegetarian that died?

Kathy   There was a big turnip at the funeral.

He claps his hands in a flourish. They both laugh.

Arthur Did you hear about the blind circumciser?

Kathy Don't tell me.

Arthur He got the sack. (*He winces, then continues.*) The blind man who got the cheese-grater for Christmas?

Kathy What?

Arthur He tried to read it but it was too violent.

Kathy Where do you find them?

Arthur I met them all on a bus last week, they were getting the free travel. (*Pause.*) Maybe I've been away so long they're new again. (*Pause.*) Some days I get lost. Do you know that? My feet think they know the way and I find myself turning down a side street that's gone. There's nothing there, just a few barrels and some old 'got-ye' in a hut watching over the cars parked where the buildings used to be. Sometimes . . . it frightens me . . . you know like in a dream . . . the sequence doesn't make sense . . .

Kathy *climbs to her feet and interrupts him suddenly, blurting the sentence out, half embarrassed.*

Kathy I love you, Arthur. At first I wasn't sure. First I was just running away from everything else. But now I know. I'll follow you anywhere, any place. I want to live in that city you carry in your heart. You don't need this place to make it real, it's dead here, finished. We could go away, together. We could be free Arthur. Out in those foreign cities you've talked about, those names . . .

Arthur No. (*Shouts.*) Why do you always say this? Why can't you let me be . . . here?

Kathy It's killing you. You're changing. Go, Arthur.

Arthur No. I'm . . . (*Quietly.*) I'm scared to go back. Fifteen years, love. In limbo – autobahns, trains, borders. But I was never homeless, always knew I'd come back. Here, at least, I know who I am. I don't have to register my address with the police. Can't you see that, love? (*He glances towards the window again.*) He's back.

Kathy   Who?

Arthur   Deignan. With her again . . . that Doyle woman.

Kathy   Sure, it's only around the corner.

Arthur   What is?

Kathy   You don't know, Arthur, sure you don't? You don't know nothing. The post office, Arthur. It's children's allowance day. He holds her book as security, gives it to her before she goes in to collect, then takes it and the cash from her when she comes out. (**Arthur** *stares at her.*) You just don't understand this city now, do you?

Arthur *is silent for a moment taking this in.*

Arthur   The bastard! I'll kill him!

He goes to move and **Kathy** *jumps up to grab him. She tries to calm him as he curses Deignan.*

Arthur   Little jumped-up bastard! I should have drowned him when I had the chance!

Kathy   For Christ's sake, Arthur, stop! Have sense!

They tussle with him trying to break free as she attempts to restrain him but gradually their struggle turns into an embrace.

Kathy   I don't want to lose you. Don't want to go back to that . . . hopelessness.

He strokes her hair, soothing her.

Arthur   There's nothing to fear, love. I've had his measure all my life.

Kathy (*softly*)   Not any more, Arthur. He's more dangerous than you think. You don't know him. How he works.

Arthur   All my life I've known him and his sort.

Kathy   For my sake, fear him.

Arthur   You're always afraid.

Kathy   Afraid for you. For the rest, I'll spit in their faces. It's so good here with you it frightens me. I keep thinking nothing this good can last.

Arthur (*stroking her hair*)   When I found you I found home again. No matter what you say. No matter if I get lost at times. With you, Kathy, it feels like it always was. There's nothing more I want now, nowhere else to go. At times it's like this whole city's in terror of something that will never happen. Let's forget them all. We have this flat and each other, there's nobody can break that apart.

Kathy (*looking up at him with urgency in her voice*)   Arthur, listen to me, they're all watching you and you don't realise it. The pushers, they hate the way you look at them. Even the kids round here, Arthur, they haven't a clue who you are. I see them dismantling that bike with their eyes, breaking it down into needles and fixes. To them all you're just an outsider. And now Deignan. You remind him of things. His kind own this city now, Arthur. He'll want to own you as well. Don't you know that?

Arthur (*laughing as he climbs up on platform*)   I own this city and you and the thousands of us who live in warrens of estates and these blocks of crumbling flats. It's ours Kathy, and it doesn't matter what titles they give themselves or what rackrents they collect, it doesn't even matter if they tear down every street so we can't recognise it. They still can't take it away from us. Because when they're rotting in the soil there'll still be thousands of us, swarming out into the thoroughfares every evening. (*He climbs down to take her in his arms.*)

Come on, no more squabbling. This room is getting us down. (*He runs his hand down to her chin and gently cups it.*) Lift up your head Kate. We'll leave the bike here for a change, walk down through our town together, yours and mine. I want to show you off.

She looks up at him and they kiss.

Kathy   You never heard a word I said, did you?

Arthur (*smiles*)   Silly talk from a silly time. (*He begins to walk across the stage with her legs resting on his.*) Dole day tomorrow, love. Bread, tea, pints of Guinness and, you'll see, work will come soon. Summer's coming. I could always knock out a living in the summer months, no matter what. Just wait. That's when it will all come back. Trust me.

Suddenly the **Friend** (*playing a petty thief*) *rushes on stage and barges against* **Arthur**'s *back, separating them, as we hear a shout offstage from the* **Porter**. **Arthur** *looks back startled as the* **Friend** *vanishes.* **Kathy** *drifts offstage.* **Arthur** *lifts the platform up again and begins to wipe his hands on a rag as if fixing his bike. The* **Porter** *races on stage and runs to the far end. The* **Frontier Guard** *follows more slowly.*

Frontier Guard (*calling to* **Porter**)   Don't bother your bollix, Pascal, you'll only be wasting your time there. (*He catches his breath and points up.*) Six hallways, two back entrances and twenty-four front doors. You might as well be pissing against the wind. We'll just wait here and watch.

Porter (*breathless*)   You wouldn't mind only they flog the stuff for a tenth of the price. (*Catches his breath.*) It's demoralising this. I don't know, years ago you used to get to chase a much better class of criminal. I'm too old for this carry-on.

The **Frontier Guard** *turns to spot* **Arthur** *who scrubs with the rag, facing away from him.*

Frontier Guard   Columbus was right, Pascal. The world is round and the same faces keep spinning back. You go and check the hallways.

Porter   What's the point? You said yourself . . .

Frontier Guard   Do it!

Porter (*resigned*)   Right.

He exits and **Frontier Guard** *approaches* **Arthur** *who has been ignoring them.*

Frontier Guard   Thought I'd seen the back of you, Arthur.

Arthur   Would be a foolish man to show his back to you, Mr Lynch.

Frontier Guard   Detective Lynch to you. Always the bitter word. Like the mother. Sorry to hear about her, Arthur. (*He pats* **Arthur**'s *shoulder.* **Arthur** *nods, accepting the condolence.*) She was a good woman, always made me the cup of tea when I had to come and take you in. But sure, you were only children. God knows yous thought yous were the toughest men in the world, but you were like babes compared to the lads on the go now. Like babes in the wood, eh Arthur.

Arthur   So you say, Mr Lynch.

Frontier Guard (*putting his arm on* **Arthur**'s *shoulder*) You wouldn't be nervous now to be seen out here talking to me, Arthur?

Arthur   You know me, Mr Lynch, I'd talk to the dog in the street.

Frontier Guard (*looking up at the imaginary windows above*) But nobody else knows you, Arthur. You should be nervous. They're watching us from up there. They're wondering.

Arthur   Shag them.

Frontier Guard   It's them shagging you I'd be more worried about. (*His tone changes.*) I think you've a problem, Arthur.

Arthur   I'm listening.

Frontier Guard   A problem of perspective. Where do you stand now? This isn't the messing you and your friends got up to. This isn't a crate of beer fecked off a lorry, or a fistfight in a lousy cinema. There is a woman back there lying in a pool of her own blood – they went for her handbag and took half her arm. There is an old man down at the traffic lights with a piece of glass stuck in his eye where the bastards broke the window of his car. That was never your scene, Arthur. I've known you since you were mitching from school. Are you with them, Arthur, or are you with me?

Arthur *turns to look at him for the first time.*

Arthur   You always took your work fierce personal, Mr Lynch. You don't give a shite if that man loses his sight. I remember you chasing me after that fight outside the Savoy. Two nights you spent sitting in the waste-ground across there, waiting for me to come home for a meal. It's still your private game, isn't it, you alone against them. You're a bit old for this, Mr Lynch. Have they no desk jobs?

The **Frontier Guard** *spits.*

Frontier Guard   Ah fuck their desks and their computers. You don't fight these bastards on a screen. I'm not ready for grass yet. Listen, Arthur, you'll need me yet. I've ears you know and you've got an acute shortage of friends in this neighbourhood.

Arthur   I'll take my chances.

Frontier Guard   Come on, Arthur, pick a side. I could use a pair of eyes, Arthur, and you could use a friend.

Arthur You were always good at using.

Frontier Guard (*sharply*) You saw a girl come in here. Don't tell us you didn't.

Arthur Your little friend might need help by now or do you not fancy the tricky corners any more?

Frontier Guard (*shouts*) Pascal, get out here. (*Threateningly to* **Arthur**.) I asked you a question.

Arthur What girl?

Porter *returns, slightly breathless. He doesn't know* **Arthur** *and presumes this is a standard questioning of a suspect.*

Frontier Guard Don't be a fool, Arthur.

Porter (*circling* **Arthur**) Have you the tax up to date on that?

Arthur Yes.

Porter Insurance?

Arthur Yeah.

Porter (*mimicking speaking into a radio*) What's the registration number?

Arthur PSI 850.

Frontier Guard You were messing with that bike like you're always doing. Now don't tell me you didn't see a girl. (*No response, shouts.*) I'm talking to you, sonny!

Arthur (*looking up*) Yes, Daddy?

Frontier Guard Don't get fresh with me. Just don't. The time for that is past. I don't know what you're doing back here, but I know it's illegal. It has to be, you look fucking happy.

Porter (*still circling*) Have you the duty paid?

Arthur Yeah.

Frontier Guard   One of these days I'm taking you down for a nostalgic visit to the station. How'd you fancy a surgical glove up the arse?

Arthur (*quietly*)   Cost me fifty guilders in any other country.

Frontier Guard   You've made your choice, Arthur. Now you sink or swim in it. Do you get my drift?

Arthur   Yes, Mr Lynch, and I know you're really saying, 'welcome home, son'.

Lights go down on the three men and rise on **Kathy** *who enters from the right, her words mingling with a recording of her own voice speaking the same words on the backing track.*

Kathy
> Grief is a knot
> That is choking my throat,
> Rage is a whirlwind
> Imploding through my skull.
>
> If only I had known
> Your life to be in danger
> I would have clawed
> My way between you and them,
>
> I would have bitten
> Into their skin with my teeth,
> I would have stubbed
> Out their eyes with my nails.
>
> If only I had shouted
> When you walked from the flat
> Or ran to the balcony
> Still naked to call you back.

The **Frontier Guard** *retreats behind the raised platform with a mask over his face. The* **Porter** *approaches him from the left and mimes handing him money as music intrudes over the verses. He receives in return a bag of white powder. The* **Friend** *approaches from the left. The following muffled dialogue takes place* *in the background while* **Kathy** *is still reciting.*

Frontier Guard What do you want?

Friend I need some stuff.

Frontier Guard Where's the money? Where's the money?

Friend I'll get it tomorrow.

Frontier Guard *gestures in dismissive refusal and exits as* **Kathy** *finishes reciting and remains on stage. The* **Friend** *is rocking the platform with her hands, shouting frantically over the loud music.*

Friend I'll get you the money! I'll get you the money! I'll get you the money tomorrow.

She shoves the platform and, as it falls, the stage goes to blackout. The 'frontier post' music begins and the **Porter**, *now lying under the platform that* **Arthur** *is standing on, begins to shine the light up and down through the bars. The* **Frontier Guard** *enters to shine his torch directly into* **Arthur**'s *face.*

Frontier Guard Passport please.

Arthur *turns.*

Arthur Sorry.

He hands him his passport which the official opens and examines.

Frontier Guard Ah Irish. Irish. Boom-boom! eh! (*He laughs.*)

Arthur I know that joke. You've made that before. It's like a dream . . . recurring. I know you. Where is this place? What side of the border am I on?

Frontier Guard What does it matter to you, Irish? Either side is a long way from your home.

Arthur What's he looking at the wheels for?

Frontier Guard Looking for? It's the rules Irish, the rules.

He hands back **Arthur***'s passport and turns to go.*

Arthur   Wait! (**Frontier Guard** *stops with his back turned.*) How long have we been here? (*No reply.*) I keep thinking this . . . happened before. I can't remember things like I used to. Have I shown you my passport already? (*No reply.*) Turn around. I know your face. I have seen you before. Why are we so long here? Tell me! (*Raises his voice.*) What's keeping us here?

Frontier Guard (*turning sharply and blinding* **Arthur** *with his torch*)   You are keeping us here.

Arthur   What do you mean? That doesn't make sense. (*Shouts.*) What country have I come from? I can't remember! I can't! Which one?

Frontier Guard   One you cannot return to.

Arthur   Why? What have I done? Had I an accident? Why can't I remember anything? How do I know your face? (**Frontier Guard** *begins to move.*) No wait! I'm talking to you!

Frontier Guard *steps out of the light and stands in shadow, stage left.* **Arthur** *stares after him, then shouts under the platform.*

Arthur   Hey! You! Where is this place? Where. . . ?

The **Porter**, *without acknowledging* **Arthur**, *switches his torch off and crawls out to cross to stage right where the* **Friend** *now stands. The* **Frontier Guard** *walks up to* **Kathy** (*who has remained a still silhouette throughout this*) *as if approaching a widow at a wake.*

Frontier Guard   You know, he was a legend . . .

Arthur *is left alone, standing on the platform.*

Arthur   It was clear until I started thinking about it. Like I've been here forever waiting for this train to start . . .

Frontier Guard I used to look up to him in school.
You know, I could have been a help to him settling in.

He walks away from her.

Arthur Can't ... it's all fading. Wait. A laneway ...
that's right, flowers between the stones ... barbed wire
... bits of glass ...

Kathy (*cries*) Arthur!

Arthur And a girl! That's right, no name, can't
remember, too painful ... I loved her, she was younger,
Dublin ...

Friend Wild like his mother, that lad.

Arthur Then why was I running ... suddenly scared?

Friend The door was open day and night, children
sleeping on the floor whenever their mothers were in
hospital. As poor as anyone here herself but she always
gave.

Arthur *clutches the belt he is wearing and lifts his hands up in
shock.*

Arthur My belt has begun to rot. Like it were
transformed back into flesh.

Friend Never begrudged him, but the life was gone
from her.

Arthur How long? I must remember. A laneway, then
what? A journey through empty streets.

Friend The lad should have watched his step.

The **Friend** *retreats and the* **Porter** *approaches* **Kathy**.

Arthur Night time ... walking for hours. From the
laneway. Why? I was going somewhere, but couldn't
leave.

Porter The real McCoy, Arthur Cleary.

Arthur   Cars abandoned, bronze statues in O'Connell Street staring down.

Porter   Always drifting from one job to the next.

Arthur   Where had everyone gone? Only one voice like a whisper from a side street . . . calling me back . . .

Kathy (*cries*)   Arthur!

The **Porter** *retreats from her.*

Arthur   Not letting me go. Had to find her . . . The night went black, the moon dim like the end of a tunnel. I'm swimming towards it, but . . . always pulled back . . . by her voice, calling. And then . . . here . . . why? Why?

Kathy (*screams*)   Arthur!

She shudders as if coming out of a dream and looks over at where **Arthur** *stands on the platform. The stage is now clear, except for them.*

Kathy   You weren't there when I woke. I was frightened.

She walks towards him and he embraces her, soothing her as he strokes her hair and they sit on the edge of the platform.

Arthur (*soothing*)   Frightened? Of what?

Kathy   Arthur . . . Tell me about it all again, where you fed the swans on the steps on a Sunday. All the places. The sounds of the names are lovely, like legends, dreams. I can see it when you talk.

Arthur (*teasing softly*)   Capel Street, Rialto, Phibsborough . . .

Kathy   No Arthur, say them. They're far away, safe.

Arthur (*quietly, soothing*)   Altona. Blankensee with little cobbled steps and terrace cafés built on jetties onto the Albe that would rock in the wake of the boats passing.

Wedel where the ships would play their national
anthems as they left the mouth of the river.

Kathy Wedel.

Arthur And the dormitories. Always the same. That
time my ribs were cracked in the strike of foreign
pickers and I lay for a week in the third bunk up,
staring at the streets of Dublin tattooed along the veins
of my wrist. The stink of Turkish cigarettes, photos of
kids, pin-ups, and always at night the same talk of
returning, even if you couldn't follow the languages, you
knew what they were talking about.

Kathy And then you came back. You never told me
why, Arthur.

Arthur (*pause*) I can't really explain it. Just happened
one night, halted at a border post. Lines of tracks,
containers stacked on sidings. I'd pulled the window
down to watch a guard shining his light under the train
when suddenly I was overcome with longing for
something ... I don't know ... something I'd lost ...
(*Pause.*) I keep thinking I've found it and it slips away
again.

Kathy A city is like a person, Arthur, it can never stay
the same.

Arthur In that limbo between states I wanted it back,
everything ... waking in the bay windows of flats with a
raw throat from drink, walking to The Fifteen Acres for
a game of ball, or back along the quays always bumping
into someone. Even when you were broke you felt you
belonged. Never felt that way anywhere else.

Kathy Arthur, we could try ... there's England.

He pauses as if trying to understand it himself as well as tell her.

Arthur (*quietly*) It could have been that way for ever,
drifting from city to city. Only something happened at
that border post. I saw my reflection in the window ...

so suddenly old, so stale with experience. I felt this panic
I couldn't explain . . . that if I stayed in the carriage I
would be damned to wander for ever across that
continent. The guard had stamped my passport and
made the usual joke. I was alone. I turned the door
handle and jumped, began to run as the official with the
torch shouted after me. I never looked back, just dodged
past shunting wagons and containers till I reached the
gates and was out into the countryside. There was
woodland, through the foliage I could see lights of trucks
from an autobahn. I kept running until I came to what
I thought was a ruined house. When I got closer I
realised it was a war monument, the shell of a building
where people had been shot. I smoked cigarettes all
night leaning against the plaque, clutching that battered
green passport in my hands. Next morning I hitched to
the nearest port, caught a ferry to Holland, a plane
from there. Island's Eye, Landbay Island, wheeling over
Swords so huge below me it was hard to believe I was
home.

On the word 'home' there is a loud bang as the **Frontier
Guard** *slaps his money-lender's book against the wall.* **Arthur**
and **Kathy** *rise. They stand as if in a doorway.*

Frontier Guard (*in Deignan's voice*)   Mrs Doyle, this is
ridiculous. I am not blind or stupid. I know you are in
there. You've had enough warnings already. I'll smash
this door down if I have to! Do you hear?

The **Frontier Guard** *sees* **Arthur**.

Frontier Guard   Still here, Arthur. (*No reply.*) Hear
you haven't been too lucky on the job front. It's a tough
one.

Arthur (*turning*)   Summer's coming, Deignan.

Frontier Guard   So is Christmas. Listen to me,
Arthur, I don't like to see a school pal down on his
luck. I've a lot of business in this block, but it's

troublesome, a lot of hassle. Time is money, you know what I mean. I'm too busy to chase it. I could use somebody, someone I could trust, to keep an eye on things for me.

Arthur Summer's coming, I'll be busy.

Frontier Guard Doing what? Mugging tourists? Cleaning kitchens at three pounds an hour? Listen, I'm not talking anything heavy, Arthur, and the money'd be good. Right, you've a few messers like the Doyles, but the rest are no problem. I mean . . . they're grateful. Genuine. Ask yourself what bank wants to know people here? If it wasn't for me, Arthur, there'd be nothing bought . . . no furniture, no clothes at communion time, no presents at Christmas, people's electricity being cut off. We're talking about people nobody else gives a shite about, we're talking about providing a service . . .

Arthur (*cutting in firmly*) Thanks anyway.

Frontier Guard (*sharper*) Think about it, Arthur. You'll be a long time rotting in that flat. It's the best offer you're likely to get.

Arthur I'll manage.

Frontier Guard Okay, suit yourself.

He turns to walk off and moves a few paces before turning back. His tone changes slightly.

Well just do this for me so. (*Opening book.*) When you see Mrs Doyle, you tell her from me . . .

Arthur Do your own dirty work, Deignan.

Frontier Guard (*sinister tone*) I don't think you realise the situation here, Arthur. This is now. It's not your mother running up and down here telling people what they're entitled to. You think you're somebody, Arthur, because you swaggered around here once. Now I'm not asking you, I'm telling . . .

Arthur *moves forward as* **Kathy** *grabs his shoulder to try and hold him back.*

Kathy   No, Arthur, no . . .

Arthur (*shouts*)   The scum of the fucking earth. You weren't born, Deignan, your mother hatched you out in the back of that filthy shop! You and that spa of a brother of yours!

Frontier Guard   It wasn't your money made my family rich, with your twist of tea and your Vincent de Paul vouchers!

Arthur *grabs the folder from the* **Frontier Guard**'s *hands and, releasing the clip, scatters the pages across the stage as if over a balcony into a courtyard.*

Kathy   Oh Jesus! No! Oh God!

Frontier Guard (*shaken but in a low voice*)   You pick up every one of those, Arthur.

Kathy (*terrified*)   I'll go, I will . . .

She moves to brush past **Arthur** *who stops her with one hand, then reaches out with the other to grip the* **Frontier Guard**'s *shirt and pull him towards him.*

Arthur (*quietly but with menace*)   Don't ever address me again, Deignan. Don't ever come near me, don't be on the same landing as me. Ever.

Frontier Guard *squares up to* **Arthur** *as if about to strike him, but suddenly flinches when* **Arthur** *blows air into his face.* **Arthur** *releases him dismissively.*

Frontier Guard   You're dead, Cleary, you hear me? And I don't strike the dead, it's not worth the effort.

The **Frontier Guard** *backs away off stage.* **Kathy** *gazes down at the loose pages.*

Kathy (*softly*)   Blowing, like death warrants, death warrants.

Kathy *steps back against the backdrop of the stage. As she speaks she tears at the black cloth and it comes away leaving a blood red background. Music begins.*

Kathy's voice (*recorded*)
    You went down steps
    Because the lift was broken,
    You paused outside
    And strolled out of my life,

    Across a courtyard
    Where housewives were talking,
    Lying between sheets
    I could hear the engine start.

As she recites the masked figures of the **Friend**, *the* **Porter** *and the* **Frontier Guard** *begin to close in on* **Arthur** *from the back of the stage with raised sticks. The* **Porter** *is laughing, a hollow, mocking sound.*

Kathy
    I drifted into sleep
    To see a horse come riderless,
    Over fields trailing
    A bridle smeared with blood,

    Towards a white house
    Where a woman stood screaming.
    As I shuddered awake
    I realised her voice was mine.

All lights die except for one flashing white light. **Arthur** *runs to his right where the* **Frontier Guard** *kicks the barrel towards him.* **Arthur** *catches it, falling backwards so that he lands with the barrel like a cushion behind him. Over intense music the* **Porter** *strikes the barrel several times as the others raise their sticks.* **Arthur** *shudders each time the barrel is struck and then hangs limply against it as the scene dissolves into sudden blackout. The stage clears and a single torch light, held by the* **Porter** *(unseen) at the bottom left of the stage, catches* **Arthur** *sitting on the edge of the platform. The* **Frontier Guard** *enters behind*

him and is picked up by a second torch beam, shone by the
Friend *(unseen) from the bottom right of stage, as he sits beside*
Arthur.

Frontier Guard *(speaking as if just going through the
motions)*   Passport please.

Arthur   Sorry.

He doesn't hand over the passport but **Frontier Guard** *still
speaks.*

Frontier Guard   Ah Irish. Irish. Boom-boom! eh! (*He
laughs.*)

Arthur   I know that joke. You've made that before. I
know you. Where's this place, which side. . . ? (*His voice
trails off in sudden fear.*)

Frontier Guard   What difference does it make? Either
side is a long way from home.

Arthur (*speaking as though going through the motions of a
dream*)   What's he. . . ?

Frontier Guard   Looking for? It's the rules, Irish.

Arthur   Have I shown you my passport already? Have
I been here before?

Frontier Guard (*slight pause*)   Yes.

Arthur (*quieter*)   Then why are we stopped?

Frontier Guard   It is the border, Irish.

Arthur   Which border? Where am I?

Frontier Guard   Don't you know by now?

Arthur (*thinks, then quietly*)   This is it, isn't it . . . as far
as you take me.

Frontier Guard   You catch on faster than most.

Arthur   How long . . . do we wait here?

Frontier Guard   Till you decide to go.

Arthur   It's funny ... so much I can remember now. Her name, the feel of her skin. She was younger, you know, far younger than me.

Frontier Guard   She was then.

Arthur   What do you mean?

Frontier Guard   So many trains run through here, day and night, in all directions, all times, coming and going.

Arthur (*eyes following an unseen train*)   Who's on that one? Where's it going?

Frontier Guard   Europe ... The future ... Her children.

Arthur   Not mine.

Frontier Guard (*smiles*)   Life goes on, you pick the pieces up. Would you have had her put on black and spin out her life in mourning?

Arthur   Do they know of me? These children?

Frontier Guard   She taught them your name like a secret tongue.

Arthur   It goes on so ... without me.

Frontier Guard   She cried, Arthur, walking the quays, praying for the courage to hurl herself in. She held you here for years, begging you to haunt her. Then she learnt to let you go, so you could pass on, not remain trapped in her grief.

Arthur   Then why am I still here?

Frontier Guard   You must let her go, not plague her dreams.

Arthur   How?

Frontier Guard   I'm only the railway guard, Irish.

There is silence for a moment.

Forget them, Irish, forget her. This is between you . . .

Arthur *slowly turns.*

Arthur   And who? (*There is no reply.*) What's out there in front of me? (*The* **Frontier Guard** *shrugs his shoulders.*) I have your face now. You've been with me all along, haven't you? (*There is no reply.* **Arthur** *waits a moment before continuing.*) What do I have to do?

Frontier Guard   Remember everything, every moment, longing, whisper, every touch you've ever known.

Arthur   And then?

Frontier Guard   Let go.

The torch light on the **Frontier Guard** *goes out suddenly.*

Arthur   Into nothing? Is there any. . . ?

He waits for assurance. The **Frontier Guard** *offers none.*

Arthur   I was always clinging on. Never able to change. (*Silence.*) It's not easy. I'm scared. (*Half laugh.*) All so suddenly precious. Every moment like a film running through my skull. Never wanted it back so badly.

He looks slowly around him, wipes his lips nervously and then stares down at his hands, before raising them slightly.

Let go.

The torch dies on him on the word 'go'. The stage is left in total darkness and briefly over the faint music we hear the sound of train wheels growing in volume for a few moments before fading away.

In High Germany

a one-act play

In High Germany was first staged by the Gate Theatre, Dublin, as part of the Dublin Theatre Festival on 9 October 1990, with the following cast:

Eoin   Stephen Brennan

Directed by David Byrne
Designed by Ned McLoughlin
Lighting by Conleth White

It was subsequently staged by the Gate Theatre, along with *The Holy Ground*, under the joint title, *The Tramway End*, on 9 November 1990.

The action takes place on platform 4 of Altona railway station, Hamburg, Germany. The time is just after midnight on 19 June 1988.

The stage begins in blackout with the crackle of a loudspeaker announcing in German the arrival of a train from Essen to Hamburg, Altona. As the play progresses there will occasionally be another distant announcement or the rumble of a train far off. The stage is minimally dressed, with just sufficient detail to suggest a German railway platform. There are two poles, one at the centre right of stage and one at the centre left, with benches attached to each. On the wall to the right is an Ausgang sign for the exit and on the left an Eingang sign for the entrance.

Eoin *walks silently on from the left and throwing his bag and sleeping bag (which are tied together) down beside the pole on the right, stares at a piece of paper furled into a ball in the centre of the stage. He is in his early thirties, wearing jeans and a leather jacket, with a 1980s Ireland soccer jersey and an Ireland scarf around his neck. He walks back towards the Eingang sign and taps his hands on it, beginning to beat louder with the growing chant.*

Eoin   Ireland! Ireland! Ireland! Ireland!

The chant and banging reaches a crescendo and he stops suddenly and turns around, walking back towards the paper and giving it a few kicks around the centre of the stage. He is muttering to himself in a country accent.

Solo it, solo it, solo it . . .

He kicks the paper ball across the stage and turns, speaking the first sentence almost to himself as he unwraps the scarf from his neck.

If only we could have clung on . . . (*Pause.*) The road from the stadium was paved with stones. Real ones I mean, thousands of them littered on the ground. Almost as many stones as Dutch supporters. Thought about those stones a lot this afternoon in that stadium when I could think anything, sweating with the heat, sweating with the fear, throat raw from shouting, hands raised . . .

He lifts the scarf suddenly and chants:

Ireland! Ireland! Ireland!

He lowers the scarf again, brought back to earth.

How would we get out of that stadium alive, down the
half miles of loose stones and away from the Dutch fans
if Ireland clung on for a draw? But really I didn't give a
shite how we got down it, I'd have faced any barrage of
rocks if we could cling on, carry on to Hamburg, (*Looks
up.*) if I could carry on back to here, not alone but as
still part of . . .

*He walks over to his bags and, sitting down, puts the scarf into
the bag. He looks up.*

In Gelsenkirchen this afternoon they had these little
scuttery trains . . . like underground trams . . . only room
for maybe forty people squeezed up.

He rises.

We boarded one, up in the concrete plaza where we'd
been drinking the local beer, around fifty of us, packed
in, and took off for the stadium. The first stop was
grand, no one on, no one off. The second stop was the
problem. There was about sixty of them . . . Dutch
skinheads . . . the real McCoy – not the fey little farts of
students we'd see in Amsterdam, all Auschwitz pyjamas
and haircuts to cure headlice – these boys were mean
bastards. Shaven heads painted orange, boots thicker
than the walls of Limerick jail, sticks in their hands, eyes
like boiled sweets from Bray that would break your
teeth.

They didn't all pack on – just as many as would fit
between us and the roof. One of them had his face
pressed against mine. I could smell the drink as I looked
at him and swallowed, then . . .

He lifts his fist.

. . . did what every decent Irishman does when in doubt

abroad ... raised my fist in the air and slagged
Brits.

He thumps his fist off an imaginary ceiling and sings.

'If you hate the Queen of England clap your hands,
If you hate the Queen of England clap your
   hands ...'

He lowers his fist and looks at audience.

The Dutch fuckers smiled, banged their sticks against the
ceiling and sang. Would we ever get to the stadium?
The train stopping and starting, nobody getting on or
off, every Irishman racking his brains.

He raises fist and sings frantically.

'Adversane England, Adversane England,
Adversane, Adversane, Adversane England ...'

*He circles the space where the Dutch skinhead would be, and
hisses urgently.*

Smile, you shagging Dutch bastards, smile.

(He sings.)
'The Queen Mother is a man, do-da, do-da ...'

(Dutch accent.) 'Ya, dodadoda!'

He presses himself up as though squeezed against somebody.

The Dutch skinner pressed against me produces a roll-
up and gestures with his hand.

He raises two fingers to his lips and shouts.

'Fur!' I didn't need Shane to translate that. I reached in,
took a lighter from my pocket and began to raise it.

*He reaches into his pocket and takes out a lighter which he holds
up. We cannot see if there is anything printed on it or not.*

Then I remembered. I'd two lighters. A plain white one
and one I'd picked up in some bar in Stuttgart ...
embossed with a Union Jack. I closed my eyes, held it

up and flicked it.

He holds his head sideways, grimacing in expectation of the blow as he flicks. He waits a second before cautiously opening his eyes and glancing at the lighter in his hand.

No thump came. I opened my eyes, the lighter was virginal white. And they say there's no God, eh.

He puts the light back in his pocket and walks backwards.

Trains . . . I've always had this dream about making a film set in a railway station. It has this secret agent, I don't know, Bulgarian or Russian or some crack like that.

He moves forward, outlining the scene with his hands.

Anyway the film opens with him breaking into a deserted flat in Berlin to photograph secret documents when he gets hit over the skull and the screen plunges into blackness followed by this blurred succession of railway tracks, until suddenly he wakes up.

He looks up questioningly at the audience.

Okay, he knows he's in a railway station waiting-room. But where? That's the question. There's just total silence, nobody about, the first glow of dawn at the grimy window above the wooden bench. Could it be France? Austria? The Transvaal? Nagorno-Karabakh? Armed guards outside, secret police, trumpet-wielding shepherds?

He lifts an imaginary fur coat to look.

A dead blonde on the platform naked except for a fur coat and a tattoo of Lenin on her left buttock?

He jumps up on a seat and mimes throwing a window open.

He mounts the bench, throws the window open, thrusts his head out and sees them . . . (*Pause.*) sheep! Nothing but sheep. Thousands of the shaggers! The camera pans back to take in the sign over his head for . . .

He jumps down and gestures with his hands.

. . . Limerick Junction! (*Laughs.*) Limerick Junction, eh?
That's how I always saw them, train stations. Victorian
relics tucked away at the arse end of small towns. One
train in the morning, one at night. Miss it and you were
fucked. And, don't ask me how, but even if you were
only going from Dublin to Drogheda you still always
wound up sitting on your arse for two hours in Limerick
Junction.

He sits down, remembering.

We saw them all on Sunday mornings when I was
growing up. On our way to Turners Cross, Flower
Lodge, Oriel Park, the Market's Field, Lourdes Stadium,
(*Blesses himself.*) St Mel's Park. Once after Waterford beat
Bohs the team bus broke down and the whole team had
to come back with us.

(*Supporter's voice.*) 'What are you doing here?' one of the
fans shouted at the manager in the queue.

(*Deeper voice.*) 'I'm getting a train ticket for the team.'

(*Supporter's voice.*) 'Jaysus, you'll be doing well, they aren't
worth one!'

*He shuffles across the stage, scratching his arse as he waves an
imaginary flag and speaks in his own voice.*

Every station the same. Sleepy officials in oversized hats
reluctantly shuffling out with a flag to wave the train on.
And always the rusting metal bridge, the placename laid
out in white stones in a flowerbed centuries ago and the
platform like a ghost town until ten minutes before the
train was due. We'd hang around the platform, Bohs
scarves around our necks, watching the little civil
servants and library assistants being shunted back to
bedsit-land by Mammy and Daddy, clean underwear in
their bags.

Not that we always had it so easy, mind you. Limerick was a hole, Athlone the same. Every local thug and headbanger convinced they had to prove they were as tough as their brothers in the metropolis were by kicking your head in.

(*Shane's accent.*) 'Welcome to Ireland.'

(*His own voice.*) Shane used to say, as we pissed down back lanes for our lives.

(*Shane's accent.*) 'They're just letting us know we're welcome!'

(*His own voice.*) It's funny, I suppose, the way train stations always fascinate me. Don't know . . . maybe it comes down to the old photos. My mother had stacks of them in an old biscuit tin under the sideboard. Meeting Daddy off the train at Westland Row, seeing Daddy back onto the train at Westland Row. How many times were strangers prevailed upon to snap them standing there, awkward together in public like any Irish married couple, a little space left for decency between them? That little space shrunk and grew in Westland Row, the train wheels coming and going, chanting over and over . . .

(*He clenches his fist, moving his elbow like a piston.*) 'You'll never go back, you'll never go back!'

He walks over to sit down beside his bag and, opening it, roots inside for cigarettes, before producing a packet of twenty.

Black '57. (*Pause.*) 1957 was when the building game collapsed. I was one, a scuttery-arsed bundle of love. Daddy was a shadow coming and going, from London, Birmingham, Coventry, a succession of registered letters with crisp English banknotes, a black travel-light bag carried in and out of Westland Row. Bottles of Guinness and Babysham for my mother the night before he'd go back and always the same song – 'And still I live in hopes to see the Holy Ground once more.'

He takes the wrapping off the packet, takes out a cigarette and puts the packet back in the bag.

It would have been so much easier for him, I know, to have just picked up his one-year-old bundle and departed to a new life through Westland Row like all his brothers and sisters had, but he refused to. He had guts, my da, I'd say that for him. Guts and dreams.

He rises.

Dreams that I'd grow up under an Irish flag, knowing I belonged somewhere, a free person in a free land. (*Smiles ironically.*) Not that he'd have said it that way, or any way for that matter. Didn't speak much, my da, just worked till he dropped off a few weeks after the Yanks gave him the brush off.

A pause as he inhales.

Their stories were like the best old films, they began and ended in railways stations. So does this one, I suppose, for Mick and Shane and me. Real stations this time, or at least big stations, Hamburg and Gelsenkirchen. Hamburg eight days ago in hope, Gelsenkirchen this evening in farewell. (*Laughs quietly.*) Not places we ever dreamt we'd wind up in when we first met, Mick and Shane and me, all five years of age, short trousers, off to school, pissing ourselves with fright. I think Mick spoke first when we were seven. It was the first time Shane paused for breath. Scrawny Shane was and short, about the same centre of gravity as a duck . . .

He throws a footballing shape.

. . . lunging in after the ball, getting more kicks off other people than he ever got at it. Captain Shane we called him.

(*Childish voice.*) 'Captain Shane Birdseye and his cod pieces.'

(*His own voice.*) It took me eleven years to get the joke.

Mick said he figured it out when he was six, he just didn't get around to laughing. Never got around to saying anything, Mick.

He jumps up on the seats and raises his fist in the air as though clutching a whip.

Our teacher, Molloy, could ask him a question, hop up on the desk in full bondage gear, canes, whips, daggers and Mick would just look at him with a complete moronic stare.

His face grows moronic as he lowers his arm.

Molloy never touched him, he'd just turn away defeated, snort some remark about planting Mick with the other vegetables in the fields, and as soon as his back was turned, without even looking down or changing expression Mick would write the correct answer down on my copy book beside him.

He jumps down and looks around him.

Jesus, how could I even describe that schoolyard now? Like a scene from centuries ago? Acres of concrete split by weeds, (*He fans his hands out slowly.*) famished gulls wheeling overhead as we were herded into line by Molloy on the top step, barking orders in Irish for us to lift our hands to touch the shoulder of the boy in front, then drop them again.

He stands to attention and lifts his hands up and down in a straight line, taking on the teacher's country voice.

'Suas, seas, suas, seas.'

He lowers his hands and uses them to describe the images.

Molloy, that rancid old bastard with a strap permanently in his hand like it was a part of him. And a bench like this . . . all the way down the concrete shed where we sat, talking, joking, laughing, eating lunch quickly . . . waiting to get out there . . . on the concrete . . . among

the littered bread and papers . . . sandals, boots, shoes,
runners scrambling, kicking out, rushing after a single
dirty plastic ball. Forty forwards with no backs or
keepers . . . coats piled up as goalposts . . . and there
we'd be, Shane and Mick and me . . .

*He mimes charging after a ball, throwing himself into the air to
head it.*

. . . in the thick of it; kicking, shoving, scrambling,
together, united, till we were caught.

*He slowly draws himself to attention and stares straight ahead,
lifting and dropping his hands, speaking in the master's voice.*

'Suas, seas . . . suas, seas . . .'

*He flinches slightly, as if expecting a blow and speaks in his own
voice.*

Touch the shoulder of the boy in front, look at his
clipped hair, watch out for Molloy pacing behind . . .
your legs still tingling, breath still heavy from that illicit
game, feet itching for the last, the perfect kick, the cup-
winning goal for Bohs.

*He breaks rank as he speaks and goes to kick an imaginary ball,
freezing himself in the stance of kicking it. He stands back and
points at the spot, speaking in the master's voice.*

'This is a ball! A what, boy?'

(*Own boy's voice.*) 'A ball, sir.'

(*Master's voice.*) 'As Gaelige!'

(*Own boy's voice.*) 'Liarod, a mhaister.'

(*Master's voice.*) 'And what do you do with it, boy?'

(*Own boy's voice.*) 'Kick it, sir?'

(*Master's voice.*) 'And what else, boy?'

(*Own boy's voice, but uncertain.*) 'Head it, sir?'

(*Master's voice roaring.*) 'Pick it up! Pick it up! Pick it up! Pick it up!'

He stoops in fear and mimes grabbing the ball up. Master's voice in staccato roar.

'Not off the ground! Use your foot, use your foot to lift it off the ground! Don't you know the first rule of Gaelic football? Solo it! Solo it! Solo it! Solo it!'

He mimes awkwardly trying to run while soling the ball, but loses control and drops it. Master's voice, infuriated.

'What arse end of the bog are you from at all, boy?'

(*His own voice.*) 'The street, sir, the city street.'

He sits down on a seat.

He had a slight cultural difficulty with me and Mick and Shane, Molloy did. The old bastard couldn't accept that we existed. Whatever the role models were in his teacher-training book they didn't include us ... or streets or soccer.

He rises, impersonating the master.

'A Brit sport, an English sport played by Englishmen.'

He drops his cigarette, smiles and stubs it out.

I wish you'd lived to see us beat England in Stuttgart, you old bastard. (*Looks up.*) Not that it mattered much. He was on the way out, Molloy. It's the mid sixties I'm talking of now. Things were looking up by then, the Taoiseach Sean Lemass was playing poker over Cafollas' café in O'Connell Street, Westland Row was being renamed Pearse Street Station and we clapped hands till Daddy came home for the last time.

He moves forward.

The American factory with the shiny gold sign at the gate was his destination, the new blue overalls, the strange feel of him coming home every evening, the travel-light bag hanging from a nail in the shed where he took his spade after tea and joined the chorus of rural accents across the ruck of hedges in the long gardens.

He cups his hands to shout in a West of Ireland accent.

'Go on Roscommon. Call them spuds, eh. It's the Kerr's Pinks you want.'

He straightens up.

They lived for the provincial Gaelic results and Leo Maguire's closing words on *The Waltons* radio programme.

Raises hands in declamatory pose to give the radio announcer's famous closing line.

'And remember if you feel like singing, do sing an Irish song.'

He moves centre stage.

Meanwhile Molloy marched us up and down the schoolyard behind a 1798 pike, hustling us to try on skirts . . . for the 1916 Anniversary pageant in Croke Park. RTE cancelled *The Fugitive* to show us the Easter Rising and we almost shat ourselves, Shane and Mick and me, watching the GPO burning, Ireland's favourite soap star, Dinny Byrne from *Glenroe*, singing 'God Save Ireland', riddled with bullets while he plugged his last few Brits.

He falls to his knees impersonating a rebel firing a revolver, then joins his hands in prayer.

We knelt down at night, like Padraig Pearse at his trial said he had as a child, and pledged our lives' blood for Ireland. It was all we lived for, to grow up and die for Ireland. But in the meantime we played soccer in the back field where Molloy couldn't find us and rant at how ungrateful we were . . .

He rises and wags his finger, impersonating Molloy.

'. . . the chosen generation free at last to live in your
own land and yet turning your backs on your heritage,
living only for that foreign game.'

He walks towards his bags and speaks in his own voice.

No different than that played by the children of my
uncles and aunts who had been forced to leave before
Westland Row became Pearse Street Station.

*He puts his bags on his shoulder as though about to go, then
stops.*

Where was the first foreign station? Liverpool Street in
'81, the time we lost in Wembley. First time the three of
us had been abroad. Wound up down in the Windmill
Theatre, of course. Down below five hundred Japs, up
on the balcony two hundred Irish supporters on our best
behaviour.

Cups a hand to his mouth and shouts.

'Get them off you, ya brasser!'

(*His own voice.*) This sleazebag in a suit kept announcing

(*A sleazy accent.*) 'Gentlemen if all noise does not cease
the girls will not resume.'

(*His own voice.*) We all shut up then for a while, till this
girl came on as the Roman centurion and started off
with the whip. Shane stood up.

(*Shane's voice with mock innocence.*) 'Jaysus, you wouldn't see
the like of that on *The Angelus!*'

He drops his bags again. His own voice.

They wouldn't give us a refund, but at least we got out
easier than we got out of Wembley. The hatred there,
the naked aggression.

He sits down on a seat.

After that it was Holland, the '82 World Cup campaign. The two–all draw. Central station, Amsterdam. Hippies with cobwebs growing out of them busking on that square outside the station where the trains stopped. The Flying Dutchman and the Bulldog to our right, the red light and Chinatown to our left. We went right for drugs and left to smoke them.

He takes a long imaginary puff of a joint.

They were the flatland years, Shane finishing off his time with the ESB, Mick up in the industrial estate, me thinking I was set up for life in that Japanese plant. We seemed to spend every night in Dublin being kicked out at closing time. (*Grins, remembering.*) The time after we drew in Holland the pub was so jammed with Irish supporters that we spilled out onto the pavement with our glasses. Next thing we know at two in the morning the squad cars arrive.

(*Shane's accent.*) 'Feels just like home, lads . . .'

(*His own voice.*) . . . Shane said. They got out and – I'm not joking, pushed us back into the pub. (*Spreads his hands in disbelief.*) I mean how much culture-shock can you take?

(*Shane's accent.*) 'I could get to like this country . . .'

(*His own voice.*) Shane said. (*Sudden sourness.*) I wonder if he has?

He rises.

After that what? Belgium, Malta in '83. They became the only holidays we took. No more scuttery stations in the bog, now it was here, following the lads, coming home like heroes with tales to tell. (*Pause.*) That time we played the Danes away in '84 Mick suffered his first intimation of mortality. We hit Amsterdam first and found the only snooker hall in the gaff. He fluked a long red.

He pots an imaginary ball and speaks in Mick's accent.

'It must be me birthday . . .'

(*His own voice as he straightens up, surprised.*) . . . Mick said in a rare moment of speech. Begob, it was too, he was twenty-six that day. He didn't mind losing his hair, it was losing the cheap Transalpino travel rates that left him stranded there. Myself and Shane hit out for Copenhagen with a spare match ticket leaving Mick to console himself.

He mimes rolling a joint.

That was when I noticed the change first. Three Kerry lads were trying to get a ticket outside the ground, looking like they'd just tied up a hayrick. We gave them Mick's one free and heard about the time they had hitched to Malta from Tralee, on the dole, to see Stapleton get the winner. Their accents so broad we could barely follow them. 'How'd you get here this time?' I asked.

(*A broad Kerry accent.*) 'Ah, the oul bus, boy.'

(*His own voice, surprised.*) The bus from Tralee?

(*Kerry accent.*) 'The oul bus from Munich, boy. Sure, half the factory's here.'

(*His own voice.*) And so they were like an invisible explosion. Buses from Munich and Stuttgart, three coaches from London, lads from Berlin and Eindhoven, Cologne and The Hague, all milling together with lads from Dublin, a green army taking over the steps of the town hall across from the Tivoli Gardens. I don't know why, but that night – after the Danes routed us – listening to all those people in the pubs scared the shit out of me, like an omen, like, I don't know, like the ground suddenly starting to slide from under you.

He leans against the wall.

It was like that time in the seventies, the time they brought Frank Stagg, the IRA hunger striker, home from an English prison. Armoured cars, lines of soldiers and tanks crossing the country with his coffin to be buried under concrete like nuclear waste with an armed guard maintained on the grave, so the IRA couldn't dig him up to give him the military funeral he wanted. Sitting in the classroom that day the three of us listened, remembering Molloy's 1798 pike, his speeches the day Stormont fell, Dinny Byrne dying gloriously in black and white on the box just a couple of years before. The whole class could feel it, all of us walking home from school in silence. Nobody needed to say it. Some bastard somewhere along the line had been lying through their teeth to us. Someone somewhere . . .

He sits down again.

We were the chosen ones, the generation which would make sense of the last seven hundred years. Irishmen and Irishwomen, in the name of God and the dead generations, living in our own land, in our own jobs, our own homes that our fathers had slaved for us to inherit. Can you understand me? Back then in the seventies. We were not brought up . . . to go. We had a choice, we . . . ah!

He rises agitated and looks around.

I knew everything was going to be different when I had to move over here, I could even cope with having to register my address with the police. But it was this station which still freaked me. I remember in my first week asking some official if I could get a train from here to Rome.

(*A German accent, holding up one finger.*) 'Nien, not for one hour.'

He drops his hand. His own voice.

Lourdes Stadium, the Market's Field. I used to come

here just to read the timetables pasted on the wall –
Paris, Berlin, Prague, Bonn, Madrid, every city stretching
out across this continent could be reached by just
crossing these platforms. I remembered those names
made of painted stones in the flowerbeds beside the
platforms and felt so cold suddenly like I'd stepped
outside something.

He looks to his left.

It was over there, three platforms down that I met
Shane last Saturday morning. Eight days ago now. Mick
had flown in from Dublin the night before, non-
committal as ever. He handed me a bottle of Jameson
duty-free and his holiday visa for America. Are you
going to stay over there illegally? I asked.

He shrugs and speaks in Mick's accent.

'Do I have a choice? Does the bear shite in the woods?'

He jumps up on a seat and speaks in Shane's accent.

'And it's hello to tonight's contestants – the Germanic
Bollox and the Quiet Man.'

(*His own voice.*) Says Shane, getting off the train from
Holland.

(*Shane's accent.*) 'Fingers on the buzzers, no conferring
please, here's your starter for ten. Are we about to: a)
Collect and press wild flowers? b) Add to our collection
of rare barbed wire or? Or c) Beat the Brits, the godless
Russians and those Dutch bastards I've to work with
and in the process suffer brain death due to the
excessive consumption of noxious substances and
solvents?'

(*His own voice.*) Stop the lights.

(*Shane's accent.*) 'Shag off, you got it in one and you've
won yourself a free trip to the Reeperbahn. Lead the
way.'

He jumps down and leans against the wall.

But we didn't go at first, we just spent most of the afternoon hanging around here, staring down at the crowds milling round the trains; the crewcut Yanks with haversacks the size of a small estate in Tallaght, the Canadians always in red waterproof anoraks with a maple leaf the size of Finn McColl's dick on the back, the little French girls that would put a horn up your back to scratch your neck.

He sits down.

We took a U-bahn to St Pauli, slagging, driving each other crazy with twenty questions. Mick had one that nearly killed us – the last three sets of brothers to play for Ireland at any level from youths up. (*Gestures as if to someone beside him.*) Give us a break, I said, I'm not a professor of history.

(*Mick's accent.*) 'No, they're all in the Irish squad, or should be.'

(*His own voice.*) That gave us the first one, it was easy enough. (*Clicks his fingers.*) 'O'Learys – Dave and Pearse. Then . . . hang on, the Bradys, Liam-o and what was his name – his brother Ray, played under-21. But who the fuck else?' We were still struggling when the train reached St Pauli.

He rises and leans forward, with one foot on the seat.

'Hughton,' I said, 'Chris Hughton had a brother played under-21. Broke his leg afterwards or was it somebody else's? For fuck sake, Chris Hughton, of all the Irishmen . . .'

He puts his foot down, the good humour gone from his voice.

Though no one said it, we all knew why I skipped him over. Black and cockney. I had fallen into the trap of the knockers. His mother was from Limerick. He could have been a first cousin to any one of us. (*Pause.*) It had seemed so odd, back in the seventies. After Tuhey, when John Giles took over for Poland. Peter Thomas was the first I think, but he'd been in Waterford since before the Normans. Steve Heighway followed, but it was Terry Mancaini that brought it home, the time Givens scored the three against Russia. The bizarreness of it, this bald cockney turning round during Amhran Na bhFiann . . .

He stands to attention, turning his head sideways to whisper in a cockney accent.

'This Russian anthem doesn't half go on.'

(*His own voice.*) It didn't seem right somehow, like a party being spoilt by gatecrashers. Our own little club, our local heroes from the same back streets as us. More and more English-born players followed, new faces and accents to be suspicious of.

That was when I still believed it back then, when they didn't fit into my vision of Ireland. It was round the time my father came home with something extra in his wage packet. Uncle Sam was going home, the tax breaks and IDA grants wrung dry. The workers staged a sit-in outside the plant. I caught a glimpse of Da on the nine o'clock news, awkward in his Sunday clothes, in a ruck of men behind the union official. There was something chilling in that for me, Da suddenly becoming a moment of history, on the screen like Dinny Byrne riddled to bits. Maybe I'd always seen him too close up, but his face on the television was like a map without names. All the toing and froing from Westland Row, the years growing ashen from chemical dust.

He moves centrestage, using his hands to describe the imaginary station.

When he looked past the official towards the camera it was like he had finally reached his destination to find the station closed down, tumbleweeds blowing down the platforms, the signal box rusted and the tracks torn up.

He stops, turning his back on the audience.

Two months later after the cortège had returned from
his grave, Shane and Mick and me sat up all night,
among the vast plates of sandwiches, drinking Guinness
by the neck. I didn't weep, it was like cold water had
entered my bloodstream. I doubted if I would ever be
able to feel again.

He turns and leans against the wall.

On the train to Stuttgart Mick produced the green Oige
card we had always known. Mine was from the German
Youth Hostel Federation, Shane's from the Dutch. We
thought we were being clever, but when we got to the
hostel there half the Irish nation had thought of the
same trick. Oul lads eligible for the free travel and
women who'd never see forty again except on the front
of a Finglas bus.

He moves forward, miming playing football as he speaks.

You know about the England match last Sunday,
Aldridge flicking it onto Houghton's head, Packy's saves,
the nerves in shreds. After the game when the team had
finally gone in, we filed singing from the stadium to face
the rows of riot shields and uniforms. Shane turned to
us.

(Shane's accent.) 'Time to vacate this town, boys.'

He jumps up onto a seat and swings from the pole.

We went to a little Spanish bar above Stuttgart. Down
below us the death pangs of the British Empire,
nourished by white bread and the *News of the World*,
could run riot on the Königstrasse. All we wanted to do
was sit there entranced, and savour it, a coming-of-age.

(Shane's accent.) 'I wonder what's Dublin like? All car
horns hooting and pubs packed I suppose.'

(His own voice.) Shane said. Toners, the International Bar,

the Hut in Phibsborough, I could imagine them all and
yet . . . you know like when you dream of something
which is so real that when you wake you still want it to
be there even as it's retreating from you. Shane went
suddenly silent. We would never really know now what
they were like that night because even if we went back
and they hadn't changed then we would have. And I
knew and I think he knew that now when we said 'us'
we weren't thinking of those Dublin bars any more, but
the scattered army of emigrants who were singing in
every bar and hotel in Stuttgart that night.

He steps down and sits on the seat.

We drank now in stunned silence. I knew we were
remembering much the same things. Winter evenings in
Dalymount, Ray Tracy hanging out of Tomaszewski's
jersey. Landsdowne Road in the years after, Brady's goal
against France, that little jinking run, Stapleton's two
against Spain in '82. And all the bedsits and flats with
faltering televisions where we gathered to scream at the
set for away games, the killer blow of that Belgium goal
minutes from time when Eoin Hand was about to
achieve the impossible dream of getting us to the World
Cup finals. (*Pause.*) But it wasn't really football we were
thinking about, it was something else, something we'd
lost, that we'd hardly been aware of. That seemingly
impossible dream we'd had of finally qualifying for
something, and coming home like veterans with stories
to tell. There's no greater feeling than the feel of going
home.

(*Shane's accent.*) 'Fuck it . . .'

(*His own accent.*) Shane said, quietly to himself.

(*Shane's accent.*) '. . . Fuck it.'

He rises, continuing in his own voice.

There would be no one to tell in Eindhoven for Shane,
no one in Hamburg for me. Oh, people in work you

could tell about the game, but not the feel of it, the sense of belonging ... no language could cross that gulf.

He steps back to look behind him.

Two Brits came in – harmless, anaemic-looking fuckers, burdened down with tattoos, terrified to be alone. They looked nervously at the tricolours wondering if they'd be served. Shane beckoned them.

(*Shane's accent, with hands beckoning towards imaginary chairs at a table.*) 'Two beers for our neighbours. The poor wee pets. Sit down here, good surs.'

(*His own voice.*) Sur is the Irish for lice, pet the Spanish for fart. They looked at us condescendingly, while being insulted in three languages. We brought them drinks and waited, knowing they couldn't hold out long. It was the third beer before they got started.

(*English accents.*) 'Robson's a poky manager. I mean England being beaten by our own second team.' 'Yeah, I believe Ray Houghton went through Dublin on a bus once.' 'Hey, what do you call five Englishmen, three blacks, a Scot, an ape and a frog? The Irish soccer team.'

He claps his hands and spreads them like an old-fashioned music hall comic, then takes the leer off his face and raises his eyebrows.

We let them rabbit on, more cocky and self-righteous with each drink. One of them carried a huge radio.

(*Shane's accent, drawn out like an imbecile's.*) 'What sort of songs do you get on that? I've one at home but it's so old I can only get old songs on it.'

(*His own voice.*) Shane said. They explained patiently to him, as if talking to a retarded child, how the radio's age didn't matter, how the Irish station probably only played old songs from the sixties. The Spanish owner behind the bar was cracking up as Mick joined in.

(*Mick's dumb, mock country accent.*) 'Begob, them's great tattoos. You know, I've the old dick tattooed myself.'

(*English accent.*) 'You what, mate, you can't have your dick tattooed.'

(*Mick's country accent.*) 'Oh, I have, I've Kerry done down the side of it. You know like, I had to induce a wee bit of length into it for the job to be done and you only see the K and Y normally, but sure like on state occasions you'll always know where I come from.'

(*His own voice.*) The Brits were dumbstruck.

(*Mick's country accent.*) 'Ah, 'tis common enough in Ireland. I was in a hotel there last week and a bloke in the gents had and N and Y on his.'

(*English accent.*) 'Where was he from, County Newry?'

(*Mick's country accent.*) 'No, Newtownmountkennedy!'

(*His own voice.*) They left shortly afterwards for some reason, shuffling moodily out into the night, clinging on to Gibraltar by their fingertips.

(*Shane's accent.*) 'I don't mind those wasters . . .'

(*His own voice.*) Shane said after a while.

(*Shane's accent.*) 'It's the ones nearer home that piss me off.'

(*His own voice as he ponders the word.*) Home? (*Pause.*) After straggling up to Hanover last Wednesday to draw with the Russians, we moved on towards Gelsenkirchen for the Dutch. There was no youth hostel in Gelsenkirchen. The nearest one I could find was out in the countryside. There was only one other Irish supporter in the gaff so they bunked him in with us. He was seventeen, just finished the Leaving Cert.

(*Young Dublin voice.*) 'Staying over here. After the games

are over. Head down to Munich to try and find some work.'

(*His own voice.*) He said. (*Pause.*) The place was full of Germans, noxious, cheerful, shrill, healthy little bastards, rising at six o'clock to play volleyball outside our window. Mick sat on the step, nursing his hangover, staring at them.

(*Mick's accent.*) 'Have them little bastards no traffic to play in?'

He moves towards the Ausgang sign and speaks in his own voice.

Being back among Germans sobered me up. Yesterday afternoon I finally went down to the basement to the public phone. Hordes of young Germans crowded around the coke machine screaming. I phoned Hamburg, the click on the line, Frieda's steady German voice bringing the present back to me.

He cups his right hand close to his ear as though holding a phone, but lets the image dissolve as he speaks.

'Frieda, are you sure? Yes, I know you're regular, an efficient little German body ... I'm only joking ... I don't know ... what can I say ... of course I'm delighted, thrilled ... just surprised. You thought it might take months after coming off the pill ... Yes, I might be back in Hamburg tomorrow night, either alone if we lose or with the lads for the semi-final there if we draw ... the lads ... you'll like them ... it's great news ... ich liebe dich, too.'

He moves stunned towards the nearest seat and sits down.

I went back up through the welter of German voices. I said nothing to the lads, couldn't tell them. I knew it will be a boy, his high Irish cheekbones, raven-black hair standing out among the squads of German children like those in front of us. Will he believe me when I try to tell him of Molloy, of the three of us scrambling for the ball in that dirty concrete schoolyard. As I stood in

that hostel yesterday in the arse of nowhere, I seemed
balanced on the edge of two worlds, neither the Dublin
I had come from or the Hamburg I would return to felt
real any more. Even Frieda's news didn't register. There
was just a gnawing in my stomach that I knew wouldn't
stop until the final whistle blew in Gelsenkirchen.

*He rises and walks towards the bag, opening it and removing the
scarf which he carefully places around his neck.*

We dressed in silence as usual this morning, wearing the
exact same clothes we wore in Stuttgart and Hanover –
superstitious now, intense. We looked at each other.
Where would we sleep tonight? Munich for the A semi-
final if we won, Hamburg together for the B semi-final if
we drew. And if we lost? (*Pause.*) Nobody wanted to even
talk about that.

(*Mick's accent.*) 'Never felt this sick before a game.'

(*His own voice.*) Mick said. We were nervous, but I knew
it was different from any nervousness we'd ever known
before. This was no longer just a match, no longer just
how long the team could stay in Germany, but how
much longer we three could remain together pretending
our lives were the same, that we were still part of the
world of our youth.

He climbs up onto the seats.

We got to Gelsenkirchen, made it to the stadium down
that avenue of stones, got past the Dutch in a mass of
orange on three sides and packed into one corner of the
crowd behind Packy Bonner's goal. There were faces we
knew from Hanover and Stuttgart, faces from Dublin,
faces we'd never known before, piled in in one solid
mass of green. And when it began we screamed and we
shouted and sang our hearts out for the lads. For Packy
Bonner, for Tony Galvin running himself into the
ground, for Frankie Stapleton suddenly old and making

us old, holding up the ball, snatching those few extra
seconds that crawled by. Paul McGrath rose at the far
post and we rose with him . . .

He holds his scarf up with both hands.

. . . arms aloft, banners flying, dreaming, praying,
watched the ball spin from the woodwork. Jesus, how
close could we get?

He lowers the scarf and grips it in his fist.

Would this game ever end? My throat was parched, my
legs trembling, my heart frightened me. An old lad
beside me tried to sit on the concrete, no longer able to
bear it. All around us forty-five thousand Dutch roared
as Gullit and van Basten stormed forth, drowning our
voices. How could we make ourselves heard? It was like
throwing stones into the sea.

*He clenches his fist and looks around as though encouraging others
to join him as he sings:*

  'Sing your heart out, sing your heart out,
  Sing your heart out for the lads.'

(*He shouts.*) Ireland! Ireland! Ireland!

(*A lower voice.*) Can the lads hear us, do they know? Half-
time came and still we lived in hope. We sat on the
steps, faces white, trying to suck in deep breaths. What
could be the slowest time imaginable? Forty-five more
minutes in the heat of the Ruhr. The lads were
knackered, you could see it in them. The Dutch passing
it around, making them run for each ball.

*He slowly hunches down on the seat and closes his eyes, drawing
himself closer in as he speaks.*

I closed my eyes, almost like a premonition, and sat
down, suddenly unable to watch any more. The seconds
pounding in my skull until I opened my eyes as the roar
went forth.

He opens his eyes and looks up.

Forty-five thousand voices like shrapnel, filling up my head, pounding off my skull. Oh Jesus, Jesus, (*Slowly.*) Jesus! Shane's hand touched my shoulder.

(*Shane's voice.*) 'It's over,' he said, 'over.'

He stands up.

I stood up among the silent men and women, their faces drained and I raised my hands.

He raises his fist and screams.

'Ireland!' I screamed. 'Ireland! Ireland!' I had six minutes of my old life to go, six minutes to cheat time. The crowd joined in, every one of them, from Dublin and Cork, from London and Stockholm. And suddenly I knew this was the only country I still owned, those eleven figures in green shirts, that menagerie of accents pleading with God. Shane and Mick stood solid at my right and left shoulders. I knew they were thinking too of the long trains back to new homes. The tunnel was being pulled out for the end of the match, photographers gathering down on the touchline. We lifted our voices in that wall of noise, one last time to urge the lads on.

He raises the scarf once more and screams.

Ireland! Ireland! Ireland!

He lowers the scarf, suddenly weary.

And then the final whistle blew, I lowered my head feeling suddenly old. The players sank down, knees pressed into the turf as the Dutch celebrated. And after a few minutes when I looked around none of us were moving as the Dutch fans filed away, muted and relieved down that avenue of stones.

He turns to look behind him for a second.

And when they were gone, we turned, solid to a man and a woman, thirteen thousand of us, cheering, applauding, chanting out the players' names, letting them know how proud we felt. I thought of my father's battered travel-light bag, of Molloy drilling us behind that 1798 pike, the wasters who came after him hammering *Peig* into us, the masked men blowing limbs of passers-by off in my name. You know, all my life it seems that somebody somewhere has always been trying to tell me what Ireland I belong to. But I only belonged *there*. I raised my hands and applauded, having finally, in my last moments with Shane and Mick found the only Ireland whose name I can sing, given to me by eleven men dressed in green. And the only Ireland I can pass on to the son who will carry my name and features in a foreign land.

I thought of my uncles and my aunts scattered through England and the United States, of every generation culled and shipped off by beef on the hoof. And suddenly it seemed they had found a voice at last, that the Houghtons and McCarthys were playing for all those generations written out of history. And I knew they were playing for my children to come too, for Shane's and Mick's, who would grow up with foreign accents and Irish faces, bewildered by their fathers' lives.

All thirteen thousand of us stood on the terrace, for fifteen, twenty minutes after the last player had vanished, after Houghton had returned, forlornly waving a tricolour in salute, after Jack had come back out to stand and stare in wonder at us. Coffin ships, the decks of cattle boats, the departure lounges of airports. We were not a chosen generation, the realisation of a dream any longer. We were just a hiccup, a brief stutter in the system. Thirteen thousand of us stood as one on that German terrace, before scattering back towards Ireland and out like a river bursting its banks across a vast continent.

He steps down from the seat and puts the scarf around his neck.

I did not need to look at Shane or Mick. We knew that part of our lives was over for ever. We had always returned together to Dublin once, a decade spent in a limbo of youth, poker sessions and parties in bedsits, football in Fairview Park on Sunday mornings before the pubs opened, walking out the long roads to Phibsborough and Rathmines on Saturday nights with six packs and dope and a sense of belonging so ingrained we were never aware of it.

He lifts his bag up on his shoulder and turns, speaking in Shane's accent.

'Italy, 1990 lads,' Shane said, 'we'll be there.'

(*His own voice.*) But we knew we won't be, even if Ireland qualify, knew we were fractured, drifting apart, with new lives and responsibilities taking hold. Jesus, we all felt so old suddenly.

(*Shane's accent.*) 'We did it,' Shane said. 'The first time ever. We were a part of it.'

He walks towards the Ausgang sign and stops, fingering the scarf for a moment and speaks in his own voice.

I walked down to platform B17 at eight p.m. this evening, found a carriage by myself, and when the ticket inspector came in he saw this scarf and nodded with a new respect. I remembered my father in carriages like that, perpetually coming home to his son in Ireland. But when I closed my eyes the Ireland I saw wasn't the streets I'd known or the fields he'd grown up in. I saw thirteen thousand pairs of hands moving as one, united by pride. I knew Frieda would still be waiting up, with my son, my future, a tiny pearl growing inside her.

'Come on train,' I said, 'faster, faster, take me home to her and to him.' The lights of a dozen German towns spread out while the train sped on. And all the way here it wasn't the wheels that were chattering, but the very network of tracks, carrying us all away from Gelsenkirchen, scattering us like seed across the continent, those steel lines chanting . . .

He sings as he exits.

'Olé, olé, olé, olé, Ireland, Ireland!
Olé, olé, olé, olé, Ireland, Ireland!'

The Holy Ground

a one-act play

The Holy Ground was first staged (with *In High Germany*, as part of a double-bill entitled *The Tramway End*) by the Gate Theatre, Dublin, on 9 November 1990, with the following cast:

Monica   Pat Leavy

Directed by David Byrne
Designed by Robert Ballagh
Lighting designed by Nick Beadle

The action takes place in a living room in the suburb of Drumcondra, in Dublin in the late 1980s.

The lights come up on a living room in Drumcondra, an old suburb of North Dublin. There is a window with lace curtains to the left with an old armchair facing it. In the centre of the room there is a large fireplace with a red perpetual lamp and a picture of the Sacred Heart above it. The mantelpiece is littered with masscards in envelopes, an old-fashioned photograph of a 1950s amateur soccer team in a frame, three scrapbooks, letters and newspapers and a mug of water. To the right is a small table and in front of that a hard kitchen chair facing the audience. On the floor behind the chair is another scrapbook, a box file and an accordion-style filing box and various scattered letters and pieces of paper with an almost empty black sack lying in the centre of it all. A few feet to the right is a huge ugly old television on the floor which we can see flickering. We can hear music and voices from it which we may recognise as a scene from Brief Encounter. *A few feet to the right of the television is the door of the room.*

Monica, *a woman in her late fifties dressed in mourning black, is standing by the fireplace putting papers into the half-full black plastic sack she is trailing in her hand. She stops for a moment and glances at the television, a sad smile coming onto her face as she becomes absorbed in the romantic scene being played out there. She moves slowly towards the set until she is bent in front of it, watching. Then with a sigh, she turns the sound down and leaning on the chair for support lowers herself onto her knees to pick up some of the papers there. She leans back.*

Monica 'Only two places the men in this ballroom want you,' Deirdre used to say. 'On your back and on your knees.' Myles was simpler I suppose, he just wanted me on my knees. 'A simple man and great one,' was what the priest said.

She rises and moves towards the fireplace, glancing back a moment at the television.

It's funny that. Not half the pleasure watching it now that he's gone. What was it Clarke said this afternoon, himself and his cronies here in their best suits praising him?

(*She impersonates the mourner's accent.*) 'Himself was very particular about the television. I never even knew there was a set in the house all these years.'

(*Her own voice.*) 'Please,' I said, trying to be firm. 'I want it brought in here.' (*She looks down at bags.*) That's when Clarke saw the plastic bags.

(*Mourner's voice, almost sharply.*) 'Be careful missus. He'd important minutes there of our early meetings. Maybe we should take the papers and his letters.'

(*Her own voice, looking over at the empty chair.*) I stood up to them Myles. You'd have never thought I'd have the courage.

(*Mourner's voice.*) 'You'll need a hand to sort them out. You'll be responsible for his memory.'

She glances fretfully over her shoulder at the armchair.

Your memory Myles? You still there? (*Pause.*) I've to keep telling myself you're gone. (*She circles the armchair, moving as if lost.*) Waiting for your footstep, looking for your shirts to wash. Hard to stop after all the years I've worn this ring.

She rubs her wedding ring unconsciously as she sits in the hard chair.

Grief, that's what they were all looking for. Me to play my part, a public tear at the church or graveside. Grief. (*Pause.*) There was a farm labourer away working in England when I was a girl. Fell to his death on the building sites. A new sergeant was in the barracks in Carlow, cycled out to his house in the rain and nearly banged the door down.

(*A gruff voice.*) 'Are you the Widow Dolan?' he shouts when the labourer's wife opens up.

(*Her own voice.*) 'I am not.'

(*A gruff voice.*) 'Well, you are now.'

(*A pause, then her own voice.*) I am too. The Widow Ó Muirthile.

She rises and begins to walk towards the armchair.

I kept remembering the night you gave me the ring Myles, that little flat I had in Portobello. The girls in the shop giggling about the great catch I'd got. And I had too, you were great. The Clonturk Celt. I remember cycling out to the Phoenix Park to watch you rising for the ball, that awful thud when skulls collided. And you came out of it unscratched at the final whistle and over to me. How proud I felt. Could never tell you.

She stands with her hand touching the back of the armchair as if searching for softness and reassurance from it.

I just reached up to stroke your hair and like a little boy you grinned. And that's what you were to me, a little boy in a big jersey clutching your shin-pads like trophies. So sweet after the rough mauling of hands I'd always known at the Metropole.

She turns and moves back to the fireplace to pick up the team photograph, then sits on the chair.

It was Deirdre in work who asked me to make up a foursome. Sunday, the 25th of April, 1954.

(*A girl's voice.*) 'It will either be a celebration or a wake depending on who wins,' she said.

(*Her own voice.*) We met near Richmond Road, at the bridge over the Tolka. *Swifty*, her boyfriend called him. He didn't know what way to turn himself. All the way up Hollybank Road, shuffling his feet.

(*She looks around, impersonating Myles' voice.*) 'Wasn't it mighty? The match, mighty?'

(*Her own voice.*) 'What match?' I said and he almost dropped. 'Who was playing, who won?' (*She pulls a face, smiling.*) The look on your face, Myles. The indignity.

(*Myles' voice.*) 'We did. Drums, Drumcondra. We won the cup!'

(*Her own voice, looking down at the photograph in her hand.*) This old photo shut Clarke up, made him stop fretting over your papers.

(*She looks up, speaking in mourner's accent.*) 'Bedad, soccer. Must have been your side of the family, missus.'

(*Her own voice, as she points with her finger.*) No. I pointed. 'That's Myles ... there in the back row.'

(*Mourner's accent, incredulous, as if humouring a child.*) 'Myles Ó Muirthile. On a soccer team. Aye.'

(*She lowers photograph and speaks in her own voice.*) 'Hurley.'

(*Mourner's accent.*) 'Oh, he'd play hurley all right.'

(*Her own accent, firmly.*) 'No. Myles Hurley. That was his real name.'

(*Mourner's accent.*) 'Didn't I know the man half my life ... ?'

(*Her own voice.*) 'I was his wife.'

She rises and moves back towards the fireplace.

I thought he was a player that night. 'Deirdre, why's he called Swifty?' I asked in the ladies.

(*A girl's voice, giddy.*) 'Because he runs around every weekend watching match after match like Matt Talbot racing between masses!'

(*Her own voice.*) We almost died laughing in the cubicle. Deirdre shuffling up and down in her dress, describing the other lads impersonating him, running with his hands in his pockets to see the kick-off of some game. 'So he's not a star. You haven't set me up with somebody rich and famous?'

(*A girl's voice, throwing her eyes up to heaven.*) 'Clonturk
Celtic, Monica. Sunday mornings up in the Fifteen
Acres, and even then he mainly plays "Left Outside" for
them.'

*She puts the photograph back on the mantelpiece and grows serious
as she moves towards the back of his armchair.*

You did me grand, Swifty. I didn't want a star. I came
out and saw you sipping a lemonade, your eyes on that
ugly cup the players were drinking from. You were like
a child left alone when all the other kids are playing. I
let you talk about them – your heroes, Rosie Henderson
and Kit Lawlor, until at eleven o'clock Deirdre's
boyfriend had to ask you to see me home.

She looks out towards the audience.

Had he ever kissed a girl? He gave no sign of knowing
how to. I didn't know what to do those first dates . . .
I'd pause outside on the steps . . . waiting . . . lift up my
head like . . . (*She raises her head.*) so he could see I was
. . . (*Her voice deflates.*) willing. (*Pause.*) Just to be kissed. I
remember the week before I met him . . . a brute of a
Galway man I had to fight off with my nails. (*She
shudders as though pushing a man off.*) Still had the scratches
on my legs the first time Myles asked me out. I
remember (*She holds her arms up to her shoulders as though
modelling a frock.*) worrying about them as I was dressing
before the tiny mirror, afraid of what he would think if
he saw them.

She drops her hands and the smile goes from her.

No, not afraid. I was afraid of nothing then. I was . . .
(*She pauses, trying to understand.*) Then why did the likes of
Clarke scare me so much before? How many hundreds
of people have I opened the door to and yet I could see
them outside the church whispering 'Which one is
Myles' wife?'

The priest made me sit in the front pew. I didn't want
to. I knew what would happen, the queue stopping as

somebody sympathised with the new secretary and the
person left staring into my face, wondering who on
God's earth I was.

*She picks up the scrapbooks from the mantelpiece and flicks through
them.*

You would have loved it all the same Myles. TDs,
councillors, the local papers. (*Pause.*) Last night I went
through them all . . .

She puts the scrapbooks into the rubbish sack.

. . . the letters cut out under the different names you
used. There was one scrapbook coded like the others,
but it was empty. Page after page I turned, before it
came to me. It was for your epitaphs Myles, the record
of your last appearance.

*She laughs sadly and places the sack in his armchair where the
audience cannot see it.*

The Life and Works of Myles Ó Muirthile, formerly Swifty
Hurley of Clonturk Celtic.

*She pats the bag as she speaks and then steps back, talking to the
armchair.*

I thought you were the silent type till the night I asked
you in for tea. Then when you talked you were like
nothing I'd ever heard. I remember all the names still,
the teams you mentioned – my favourites were Bray
Unknowns.

*She moves around to the back of the chair, touching it with her
fingers as if seeking a response.*

I could imagine them like a lost tribe tramping down
the Sugar Loaf once a year in grass skirts for the first
round of the Cup. You had a smile that night, Myles,
that could knock a girl down when you talked . . . teeth
so white. And you even forgot to be awkward.

She kneels down almost dreamily beside the armchair.

And while you talked I came and knelt beside you, leaned my head against your knee. Felt your fingers twisting little strands of my hair after a while.

(*Myles' voice.*) 'Bridesville,' you said softly, 'Bridesville.'

(*Her own voice.*) This is it I thought. I'll raise my head now and he'll kiss me. This is it.

(*Myles' voice.*) 'Bridesville,' you said one final time.

(*She lifts her face to be kissed, speaking in her own voice.*) 'Bridesville,' I replied like a vow, holding my mouth up to yours.

(*Myles' voice.*) 'Lost to Dundalk once in the first round.'

(*She sits on the floor, deflated, speaking in her own voice.*) I opened my eyes, you were staring at the ceiling.

(*Myles' voice.*) 'Shields scored a lovely goal for them.'

(*Her own voice.*) That was it. For months. Lifting my head, waiting, wondering was anything wrong with me? Was there anybody else or did he just not know how to break it off? It felt so nice at first, like I was a piece of porcelain. But I wasn't. I was a woman of twenty-three and I wanted a man.

She rises and moves across towards the television.

'Bring me along,' I said one night, 'the next home match you're going to.' (*She laughs.*) The pleasure on your face Myles. You closed your eyes, I think you saw us for ever in the moonlight, hand in hand watching Bohemians play Shelbourne. Then you opened them again and I saw your fear.

(*Myles' voice.*) 'What would *the lads* say?'

She leans forward to raise the sound on the television for a moment so we hear a snatch of dialogue, then lowers it again and straightens up.

It would have been easier to get him up the aisle than

in that turnstile. I loved those lads I met the Sunday he finally brought me to see Drums away to Bohs, his friends at the Tramway End. The way they slagged him and made me welcome. Myles blushed till his neck was like the Red River Canyon, then forgot about everything and roared his head off at the Drums' defence. 'Come on,' they said after the game, 'we'll finally get this fellow inside a pub.'

She grips the top of the hard chair as though it were an arm.

He trudged along behind them as they made up to me. The jokes and songs they had, oh they were lovely lads, and in the pub I gripped Myles' hand to let him know he was the pick of them. 'Sing Myles, sing,' they said and finally he did, in the middle of the floor, clutching his lemonade.

(*Myles' voice, singing.*)
  'And still I live in hopes to see
  The Holy Ground once more.'

(*Her own voice.*) 'Fine girl you are!' his friends shouted the chorus and winked at me. 'Myles, what's The Holy Ground?' I whispered.

(*Myles' voice.*) 'Ireland,' he said, 'the holy land of Ireland.'

(*Her own voice.*) And now a song from Monica, they demanded. I gripped his hand and closing my eyes, sang what my mother used to sing me to sleep to.

(*She sings.*)
  'Oft in the stilly night
  Ere slumber's chains have bound me,
  Fond memories bring the light
  Of other days around me . . .'

She sits on the word 'stilly', her face suddenly drained, her voice faltering away to a whisper.

The stilly night, Myles. The stilly night. I overheard two of them at the graveside.

(*Mourner's harsh accent.*) 'Cold as a fish. Not an ounce of grief in her.'

(*Her own voice.*) Didn't I grieve enough for you in the stilly night below me here on your knees before the perpetual lamp of the Sacred Heart? Lying awake through the joyful and sorrowful mysteries, wondering. Then half asleep, hearing your foot on the stair. One step, two step, the bogeyman is coming. Waiting for the pause on the landing. Would you turn the handle?

She rises quickly as if banishing the thought and walks to the right of the mantelpiece to get a cardigan, which she pulls on, shivering as if suddenly cold.

Who would have thought back then? The day we walked all the way out to the Poolbeg lighthouse with you not speaking. Me thinking, this is it, we're going to break up.

She crosses to the fireplace.

My heart was down in my boots because . . . you made me feel special Myles, not just a heifer at a mart. You turned to me – I'll never forget that stare – like you were about to commit murder. Then I knew suddenly. You were helpless. You didn't know what to say. 'Myles,' I said. You closed your hand over mine.

She joins her hands and bringing them up to her chest, rubs them against each other, looking suddenly deeply vulnerable.

And when you took it away I felt the shape of the box. I didn't know what to say . . . so I said 'yes'. Just like that. Looked at you there, like you were about to blubber and I loved you, Myles. You were my child, under that big frame, and I swore I'd look after you and keep you from harm.

She lowers her hands.

He had everything planned. He was good that way – deposits, instalments. I didn't know the half of it. There was no need for me to. This house within a roar of Tolka Park, this same furniture ... all calculated, down to the shilling. The table and chairs already bought. The beds from his mother's farmhouse. The cradle that had been his.

Her voice grows suddenly cold as she reaches a hand out, rocking it in her imagination.

I hated that. From the day he showed it to me, upstairs in the spare bedroom, alone in the corner ... the bare floorboards, the window with no curtains. I don't know why it scared me so much. He'd kissed me a dozen times and now suddenly it was there, waiting to be filled. I wanted to tell him to put it away, take it out when the time came. But he stared at it, like ... an obsession and I could say nothing.

She withdraws her hand in horror.

I dreamt of it that night. Rocking by itself, empty in an empty room. (*Long pause.*) Empty in Siobhan's room. It was the most crazy thing ... when the priest was reading the burial rights, I looked up, half expected Siobhan to be there and little Simon, tiny figures at the back of the crowd, waving goodbye to their daddy. Why ... it's been years since ...

Her voice falters out, agitated, and she picks up the second black plastic sack, moving again as if lost, looking for something to put into it. She drops the sack and sits on the hard chair, twisting the ring on her finger.

Our wedding night he was so gentle. Only other person I ever slept with was Deirdre, sharing that little flat when we first came to Dublin. I missed her now and the girls in work, fingering his socks, wanting to ask someone how often to wash his pyjamas. The little names we had for each other, the way we'd make excuses to go to the bathroom. Sometimes we were so polite we'd start giggling at the table. So little I knew about men really, so little if anything he knew about women. He came in from a match and looked at my face.

(*Myles' terrified voice.*) 'Oh, my God, are you in pain?'

She rises, speaking in her own voice as she moves towards his armchair.

'Myles,' I said, 'it's my friend has come.'

(*Myles' voice baffled.*) 'Deirdre?'

(*Her own voice as she stands in front of the chair.*) 'My time of the month Myles. Women bleed, it's painful, do you understand?' I could see his face clouded.

(*Myles' voice.*) 'Did I do wrong? Does that mean. . . ?'

(*Her own voice.*) 'It takes time,' I said. 'Time.'

(*Myles' voice.*) 'When can we try again?'

(*Her own voice.*) Those few days Myles, you were someone else. Then, when it was time, you were rougher, I wasn't ready. It was . . . more like a challenge. It hurt. (*Pause.*) And every time it hurt more.

She recovers herself and glances down at the old newspapers at her feet.

Gusey Goose and Curly Wee. They were Simon's favourites. Waiting all day for his daddy to bring home the *Irish Independent*. Ah, but my stories were better than any cartoon. Siobhan never tired of hearing about when I was a young girl.

She tentatively moves to address the front of his armchair.

'We're still so young. A year isn't long. There's doctors. A check-up . . . for us both. Myles?'

She looks out across the chair towards the audience.

I went alone those first two times. Felt guilty just sitting in the queue. The second time there was a pregnant

woman across from me. Couldn't bear to look at her . . .
it shamed me.

(*A booming, refined accent.*) 'Why doesn't your husband
come, Mrs Hurley?'

(*She laughs, speaking in her own voice.*) Oh, it was years
before I got the joke.

(*Refined accent.*) 'Why doesn't your husband come?'

She moves to the window, gazing out through the curtain.

The dreams of Monica.

She turns back to gaze at the chair.

You were my dream Myles, the only dream I ever
knew. This little house in Drumcondra, the crooked
street-lamps, the funny dog next door. All I had ever
been taught to dream of. Deirdre and the girls fussing
when I left work, demanding that I bring the first child
down for them to see. They were your dreams too
Myles, putting your bicycle in the shed, black boots
running down to greet you, the excited squeal of voices.
And you on the sideline one day roaring Simon on, him
living out your dream in the black and green of
Clonturk Celtic.

She crosses the stage.

Maybe I should never have badgered him to go. Might
have been better . . . if we'd never known. Sitting in that
chair when he came back.

*She walks back nervously to stand with her fingers spread inches
from the back of the armchair.*

Shoulders so stiff. I stood behind him. And I was afraid
to touch his arm . . . like it was coiled up, waiting to
smash something. My little boy was gone, so deep in
there he could never come out. I didn't want to see his
face, afraid of what I'd see in those eyes.

(*She grips the chair, imitates his harsh voice.*) 'You call that a doctor? Oul Jackeen, trained in England. West British pup!'

She backs away from chair.

That was all you said Myles, you never mentioned it again. But you rarely mentioned anything now. That silence, both of us sitting here . . . you in your chair, me by the fire, laughter of children in the lane. Oh, if you could only have screamed Myles, I could have run to you. But you just ate your dinner in silence and were gone. Meetings, committees, training. You were like a savage on the football field then somebody told me once. Blind courage they called it. It was blind rage I knew. You'd come home, cuts on your forehead, bruised eyes. You'd strip to the waist in the kitchen – I never saw you naked. Once . . . your face streaked with blood . . . I tried to help you.

She raises her hand as though holding a cloth to his head.

You flinched when I touched your forehead, stared at me. Oh Good Jesus, Myles, I'll never forget that look.

She shudders and moves to television, watching it for a moment with no sound, then straightens up, speaking in Deirdre's voice.

'Look at the state of you,' Deirdre said, 'dressing like an old woman and you only twenty-seven. It's that queer fellow has you this way.'

(*Her own stiff voice.*) 'That's my husband you're talking of, and I don't see anyone in a hurry to throw a ring around your nose.'

She sits down in the hard chair.

I had to say it to her. Lord I was desperate to talk to someone but I still carried his name. She went to England after, never saw her again or any of them. What could I have said to them? It was the time, it was our duty. Children on the street, children in prams. Balls bouncing off walls, skipping ropes in the lanes, trolley-car wheels sparking on the pavement. Every sound taunting the pair of us. Did I even think of leaving him? Where would I have gone back then? What welcome awaited me in Carlow? What scuttery room in Cricklewood, looking over my shoulder terrified to meet somebody I'd know? I had everything I had been taught to pray for ... except a child and the love of a man. I prayed to win that back, with all my heart, all my soul.

She rises and moves to centre stage.

What did they say to him down at training that night? It was just a joke I'm sure, some tiny slight.

(*Joking male voice.*) 'No young centre forwards yet, Swifty? You'd better get the lead out of your pencil!'

She looks towards the door as if he had entered and was walking past her.

I knew by your face when you came in. Waiting for you to give me the boots as usual to clean. You went out to the shed instead, hung them there on a nail. 'What's wrong, Swifty?' I said.

(*Myles' voice, furious.*) 'My name is Myles! And it's Ó Muirthile!'

(*Her own voice, distressed.*) Ó Muirthile! (*Pause.*) I never saw you handle those boots again.

She starts packing the loose papers on the floor into the plastic sack. She picks up the accordion folder and putting it on the chair, glances at the papers inside it. She straightens up to look at the audience.

You know the Yanks you see in O'Connell Street on Patrick's Day, always wanting to meet the 'Little People'. If they only knew, they wouldn't have far to go. In the door of the GPO, second hatch on the right after the statue of Cuchulainn. Myles and thousands like him, little people in little jobs, lives bounded by foolscap paper and elastic bands.

She puts the folder into the sack with the other papers.

There was no harm in him, all he ever wanted to do was hold his head up like any other man. You couldn't think of him opening his mouth to anyone. He was made for that life as much as I was. The longing we shared that we could never speak of. Sweet Lord, the ache in my belly like a phantom pain, the dreams of morning sickness like honey on my throat.

She grips the chair for support.

That night you hung your boots up I knew you were awake. I was praying in the dark, the Little Flower, my namesake, St Monica. Begging them to show me how to win back your love. I traced my finger lightly down your hip bone.

She cannot stop herself shuddering as she speaks slowly in a tone almost as if she was praising him.

That was the only time he ever struck me.

She crosses to the window and looks out.

'The Dreams of Monica.' You'd sneer when you'd say it. A home, someone to love, a child . . . (*Her voice grows more desperate.*) Myles it doesn't even have to be ours. We could . . .

(*Myles' voice as she turns.*) 'Are you mad, woman! Don't think I don't hear you, up in that spare room talking away to yourself!'

She fights to put herself back together.

That's what I was, a crazy woman inventing children for herself. Oh, God forgive me, but who else had I to talk to from dawn to dusk? What priest wants to hear? The coughing and shuffling of pews on a Friday night, people wanting to be home for their tea, the face like a

blurred ghost in that little mesh of light in the
confessional.

She crosses the stage and resumes packing papers away.

I'd liked his friends I'd met at the Tramway End.
Simple honest lads who made me laugh. But those lads
were gone and forgotten now like the Leinster Senior
League.

She straightens herself, letting the sack slip from her hand.

It was the Legion of Mary now and the Men's
Confraternity. The first night he was like a man on a
date, so flustered and worried he even spoke to me.

(*Myles' voice.*) 'Am I presentable, woman, or do I look a
show?'

(*Her own voice.*) The thrill on his face when he came
home.

(*Myles' voice.*) 'I'm keeping the minutes, they know they
can trust me!'

(*Her own voice.*) It seemed to make him happy again, and
I was glad for him and proud. (*Pause.*) Proud and alone.
Reading women's magazines furtively when he was out,
waking up scared he'd find them or the photo of
Deirdre's little girl hidden among the old tins of Brasso
and paint in the shed. The only letter she ever sent.
What could I have written back? About all the years
that followed? All the Ash Wednesdays and Good
Fridays? Having my dresses inspected and make-up
banned. And every Sunday walking to Mass, feeling him
put his hand stiffly in mine.

(*Myles' voice.*) 'That new priest is a pup with his Vatican
Two. We're moving the committee lock, stock and
barrel.'

(*Her own voice.*) 'Where?' I asked.

(*Myles' voice.*) 'Here! Our own living room. Mr Clarke,
the chairman, asked for a volunteer and everyone looked

at me. That's trust for you! They're important people.
Don't speak unless you're spoken to. Just take their coats
and stay out of the way.'

(*Her own voice, as she moves around demented.*) I scrubbed the
lino in the hall, I washed the step, I ran to the mirror
like a woman demented. So long since anyone had been
to the house, I had almost forgotten how to hold a
conversation. At nine o'clock I served tea to the men
and women here, who peered at me like an unclean
animal.

She approaches the back of the chair, anguished.

What had you told them Myles? (*Pause.*) You'd told
them nothing. Did I exist at all? When we were alone
you'd talk to the evening paper.

She resumes packing as she speaks in his voice.

'*The 70s will be red!* Over my dead body. It's no wonder
the country's destroyed with the like of them plays. We'll
have a picket on that.' (*A snort.*) 'A doctor on the
censorship board? Encourage every class of pornography
so they can legalise the pill and make money on
prescriptions for it!'

(*Her own voice, approaching the back of the chair again.*) Oh,
you thrived on that anger, touring bookshops, being
abused by cinema queues. No lover could have given
you such pleasure . . .

*She grabs the chair suddenly and violently swings it around so the
audience can see the plastic sack of papers sitting in it.*

. . . no goals by Kit Lawlor or Rosie Henderson!

A pause as she goes to sit on her own hard chair.

Why were you so frightened of change? Any change,
anywhere. Hoarding things in the shed, things you'd
never use again. And I was worse, startled on the buses
when the conductor asked for the fare as though I

hadn't even expected him to notice me there. Who would have thought me capable of anything? (*Pause.*) But the night he taunted me about them, I murdered Siobhan and Simon in their sleep, over and over in my dreams, their little faces turning blue under the pillows. 'I will not go mad here,' I said, 'I will be sane, sane.' I was sane for twenty stale years. (*She looks towards the chair.*) If I could kill the children that I loved, Myles, even if they only existed in my head, then I should easily have been able to murder you.

She is silent for a moment, recovering herself.

A great man, the priest said. Great, but I could barely recognise him now.

She rises, approaching his chair as if challenging him with the words as she speaks in a country accent.

'Bravo to an tUsual Ó Muirthile for his letter about the pill. It's men like him we need to stand against the foreign tide of muck – A Mother of Five.'

She stops, speaking in her own voice.

Nobody could even talk to you now, schisms and intrigues plotted in our living room. The scrapbooks started for the letters to the papers under different names. When your writing grew too familiar you made me copy them. 'Cork Mother of Five', 'Dublin Mother of Seven'. Every time he made me sign myself that I cried.

She turns back to grip her own chair for support.

Every other humiliation I could take, I had been obedient like my parents had taught me, but in my room I cried and in the shops I heard the whispers.

She sits down, pausing.

It was an accident the first time, rats in the shed. Myles had the poison on a shelf in the kitchen. My elbow

slipped. It covered his cabbage like a fine dust. I was
about to throw it out when I stopped. I looked inside
and saw him crouched at the table like an alarm clock
about to go off. I wiped most of the poison off, poured
his favourite gravy and served it to him. Just a speck
left, Myles. No real harm meant, like a waiter spitting
into the soup. But God, that night the thoughts I had of
you lying stiff in the spare bedroom. Autopsies and
squad cars coming for me. All the next day I thought of
prison. Would it be any different from the way I lived
now? (*Pause.*) I could have gone out at nights, bingo or
. . . but I'd have felt so strange there, so . . . exposed. I
felt safe here in this house, for years it was all I'd
known. Watching television in the kitchen, hunched up
(*She hunches her shoulders.*) like a cat with my finger near
the knob and the sound turned almost off in case he'd
return. I loved the company of it. Almost died the night
I heard his voice there.

(*Myles' voice.*) 'Marriages are made in heaven, divorces in
hell.'

(*Her own voice.*) That time around the elections and the
divorce referendum, TDs and senators calling to the
door, promising him anything for his seal of support.
That photographer who snapped us for the *Sunday World*.
I remember blinking in the light and looking back into
the kitchen where Clarke and the others watched. Oh
God, I felt so unclean and bewildered, wanting to hide
away with the photo of Deirdre's little girl in the shed.

She rises and walks towards the fireplace, resuming her packing.

Then the elections finished . . . it was like the news on
the telly . . . the wars they stop showing so you forget
they're going on. (*Pause.*) That was you Myles, letters
unprinted, phonecalls not returned.

She stops packing and looks up.

I've never harmed a hair of anyone. So what made that

thought return?

She moves back to her chair, thinking and then sits.

It was that young mother in the supermarket with the
freckled little girl, the image of Deirdre's. She'd pinned
a little badge on the child. When she saw me reading it
and I smiled she smiled a little defiant smile back, as if
to say we'll beat them, we'll live our own lives yet. That
arm (*She raises her right arm.*) I would have cut off just to
go for coffee with her like I've seen other women do, to
play with the little girl, to talk to someone. (*Pause.*) The
badge on the little girl said 'Spuc Off'.

She rises, suddenly overcome with laughter that is close to tears.

'S.P.U.C. Off.' I started laughing, the cashiers looking
up with startled eyes. 'Spuc Off! Spuc Off!' Oh God, I
laughed, the tears down my face. A space cleared
around me and the young woman touched my elbow.

(*A concerned female voice.*) 'Are you all right. Can I get
anyone . . . your husband?'

(*Her own voice.*) 'My husband is dead,' I said, 'thirty years
dead. Swifty Hurley, he was a good, simple man, a
footballer.' I left the shop and almost ran home. I felt
the whole street was looking at me. I took the poison
from the shed, put it above the cooker and made his
favourite stew.

She cries out softly.

Oh Swifty, my only love! You were my husband, what
would I be when you were gone?

She sits down in the chair.

All the things people kill for. Money and God and
countries. I killed for companionship, can you not
understand? Those rough women in prison, they didn't
frighten me any longer. Four of us crammed in a cell, at
least they would have to talk to me.

She rises again and picks up the now full black sack on the floor, speaking in mourner's voice.

'You'll be responsible for his papers, Mrs Ó Muirthile. When can we call for them?'

(Her own voice as she carries the sack over to the door.) 'Eleven o'clock on Tuesday Mr Clarke,' I said. Remember Myles, the binmen are always gone by half-ten.

She exits to dump the sack outside and then re-enters.

Even Clarke and his friends spuc-ed off on you these last months Myles, new offices down town, computers and spokesmen in smart suits.

She lifts the second sack from the armchair and begins to cross to the door again.

They left you alone to struggle with your own Calvary. Wandering the streets with nobody heeding you, having rows with young people sniggering on the bus home. How long would it take the poison to work? I threw it out the next morning but it was there inside you. I wanted to tell you, to warn you, but ... Myles, all these years we've barely spoken. You'd come home late and I'd hear you down here singing old hymns to yourself.

She pauses at the door and looks back in.

This was when you finally needed my help, an overwrought little boy blubbering away to yourself. But you had killed every feeling inside me until I just lay there numb.

She exits to dump the sack and comes back to stand in the doorframe.

I woke on Tuesday and knew something was wrong. The little sword of light under my door almost paled with dawn. And every step I took seemed a descent into nightmare. I stood outside this door, Myles, and realised ... I wasn't afraid you were dead, I was afraid you might still be alive. You were slumped here in front of the perpetual lamp, (*She looks down at the carpet.*) a grotesque, pitiable figure. All the years in the GPO, Myles, the second hatch on the right after the statue of Cuchulainn. It wasn't Rosie Henderson I saw now, but that statue of a warrior dying, tying himself to a rock. For half an hour I stood in this doorway like the men of Ireland, afraid to approach, not daring to call your name in case you'd look up. Then ... I went walking through the streets in my slippers and dressing gown.

She crosses the stage to stand beside his armchair.

Outside the Mater Hospital two nurses appeared. They brought me inside and phoned an ambulance. 'Was it the rat poison?' I kept asking. 'The rat poison?' I wanted to be charged, to be taken away.

She pauses, trying to remember the word.

What was it the doctor called it? 'Warfarin.' I think that was the name.

(*A strong male voice.*) 'Your husband died from a clot to the brain. The man had a history of thrombosis, he'd take treatment from nobody. Rat poison contains Warfarin that prevents clotting and thins out the blood. If you did give it to him you probably lengthened his life. Go home now Mrs Ó Muirthile and keep your mouth shut.'

She sits down in his armchair for the first time.

Sweet Jesus Myles, what sort of wife was I? I couldn't make you happy in life and I couldn't even send you to your death. They thought it was for you I was crying but it was for me. Because how can I cope thrust out into the world, how can I learn to watch that (*She glances towards the television.*) without hunching up beside it, to walk out into the evening like an ordinary person? To learn to play bingo and sit in the park, to chance a conversation with a kind person on a bus?

She seems to sink further and further into the armchair.

The doctor sent in an old nun in white robes to comfort me. She pressed her hands in mine. 'Pray,' she said. Those kind eyes she had, she made me feel warm. 'Our Father who art in heaven,' she began. I closed my eyes and thought of God. I saw him there kindly ... like my own father beckoning, but suddenly you were there beside him, Myles, righteous and stern.

The lights have gone down until there is just her figure lost in a dim spotlight.

I tried to pray but nothing would come. You've stolen my youth and left me barren, you've stole my gaiety and gave me shame, and when I die I will die unmourned. But I could forgive you Swifty, everything except that ... seated there at the right hand of God, you had stolen my Christ away from me.

The set fades into darkness.

Blinded by the Light

a comedy in two acts

For George, naturally

Blinded by the Light was first produced by the Abbey Theatre, Dublin, on the Peacock stage, on 6 March 1990 with the following cast:

Mick	Donal O'Kelly
Siobhan	Alison Deegan
Scottish gentleman	Wesley Murphy
Shay	Eamonn Hunt
Bosco	Frank Kelly
Ollie	Gerard Byrne
Pascal	Phelim Drew
Elder Stanford } *two Mormons*	Enda Oates
Elder Osborne	Michael James Ford
Lily	Máire Ní Ghráinne
Jack	Maurie Taylor
Mr Lewis	Kevin Flood
Sean	Owen Roe

Directed by Caroline FitzGerald
Designed by Chisato Yoshimi
Lighting/Production Manager Trevor Dawson
Sound by Dave Nolan

The play is set in a Dublin bed-sit. Apart from Joe Dolan, the choice of all other music is optional and may be updated within the same range of impeccable bad taste.

Act One

Scene One

In blackout we hear Joe Dolan finish singing 'Make Me an Island'. The song dies, followed by momentary static after which, seemingly from below the stage, Joe Dolan starts to sing 'The House with the Whitewashed Gables'. The stage is in darkness through which we can discern the outline of **Mick***'s untidy bed-sit, crammed with stolen hardback library books. The top half of the back wall may be in the form of a gauze, which appears solid when the bed-sit is ordinarily lit, but is transparent when the bed-sit is in darkness and the hallway (running behind it) is lit. However this corridor can also be left totally unseen if director and designer see fit.*

We hear a door open and the soft click of a light switch in the hall, so that a low arc of light appears beneath the doorway of the bed-sit from the corridor behind it, or else the gauze is lit up so that we can see the outline of figures approach. There is the clatter of footsteps, the clink of bottles and the drunken murmur of **Ollie***,* **Pascal** *and* **Bosco** *in the corridor, all of whom have heavy Drogheda accents.*

Ollie   Jaysus, I'm a tad sick of Joe Dolan! Who's the header downstairs always playing him?

Pascal   Lord knows. He never goes out. That oul acid's a bad man.

There is the sudden explosion of glass as bottles are dropped and smash on the floor.

Pascal   Buck it, Bosco can you not hold your drink at your age?

Bosco   Not in them plastic bags from the off licence. They make them fierce thin. You'd miss the oul brown ones.

Ollie   We'll be a tad short of drink tonight.

There is a jangling noise as **Bosco** *searches for his keys. The front door opens again with a thunderous noise.*

Shay (*in a voice filled with irritation*)   Jaysus, not Joe Dolan! I'll blast that spacer out of it! (*He strides up the corridor, holding a tall object.*) Is he in yet? (**Shay** *hammers on the bed-sit door.*) Where is he at all? Does he not know he'll have to be up for work in the morning? (*Pause.*) Well, shag him anyway, yous can have this so. Do yous want it?

Pascal   Never get that bucking thing on the provincial bus.

Shay (*annoyed*)   What's wrong with it? Solid bleeding steel, fierce useful too. Ah, suit yourselves. I'll show this bastard downstairs.

We hear **Shay** *stomp upstairs as a key is turned and the other characters exit into* **Bosco**'s *room, the unseen door of which would be directly opposite* **Mick**'s. *As* **Bosco**'s *door closes and the corridor light switches itself off we hear Lou Reed's 'Walk on the Wild Side' being switched on loudly by* **Shay** *upstairs, the choruses of both songs merging. The front door opens, quieter now and the hall light comes on again.* **Siobhan** *laughs in the corridor.*

Mick (*low, drunken voice*)   Say nothing to nobody in this madhouse, just follow me.

Siobhan (*incredulous laugh*)   You keep it indoors?

Mick   Sure, you'd have to. It's a vintage model. One speck of rust could knock its value in half.

The bed-sit door opens and **Mick** *and* **Siobhan** *not so much walk as stumble into the room which is now lit by a shaft of light from the corridor. Neither is too sober. There is just enough light to make out their movements.*

Mick   Caution is required. Hands and knees only from here on.

He sinks to his knees, clinking the bottle in his pocket, and with another incredulous giggle **Siobhan** *joins him and follows* **Mick** *who crawls across the worn carpet towards a bedside locker. He stops so that she almost knocks into him.* **Mick** *opens a drawer and removes something so small that the audience cannot see what it is. He places it on the floor and points towards it as* **Siobhan** *peers down.*

Siobhan   I've walked a mile and a half to see that?

Mick   It was worth it, wasn't it?

Siobhan (*quoting him*)   'Vintage model. Family heirloom.'

Mick   You asked if I had a car. Sure didn't God give you legs. What do you want a car for?

Siobhan *kneels up, swaying slightly, to look at him.*

Siobhan   You were going to give me a ride in it.

Mick   I don't remember anything about 'in it'.

Siobhan (*darkly*)   Well, a lift home then.

Mick *kneels up as well, the jokiness gone from his voice.*

Mick (*softly*)   You don't really want to go home, do you?

There is silence between them for a second.

Siobhan (*softly*)   Well, maybe not just . . .

The room is suddenly flooded with light by **Shay** *who stands in the doorway, holding an uprooted bus-stop pole in one hand. We see the bed-sit properly for the first time. The top of the wardrobe has a pyramid of empty Ovaltine tins, while a number of golf clubs lean against one wall and a guitar slumbers in one corner with four strings. The only armchair is inhabited by a family of quite grotesque soft toys. Over the single bed an ITGWU 'Strike On Here' picket has been hung up and underneath it there is a poster of the Irish soccer team framed by a green-and-white scarf. To the stage right of the bed there is a locker and to the stage left of the bed a chest of drawers has been constructed against the back wall. This chest of drawers is actually a hollow cavity which* *opens out onto the back stage area, with a secret sliding panel on top. There is an opening in the wall, stage left, hung with plastic strips as if leading into a shower unit and a curtained window in the wall beside it. In the other wall, stage right, there is an old-fashioned fire-place, constructed so as to give the illusion of flames when a fire is lit. There is also a small table and a battered sofa. Books run in a long row on the floor along the walls on all sides, yet the bed-sit is neatly kept in a haphazard way.*

Shay (*ignoring* **Siobhan** *who kneels, startled*)   Where have you been till now? Don't you know you've got to be up for work in the morning? You needn't think I'm phoning in for you again. (*Slightest pause.*) So, do you want a bus stop or not?

Mick (*rising in restrained annoyance*)   Shay . . .

Shay   Solid steel. Where would you get the like?

Mick *removes a long overcoat from the coat stand beside his bed to reveal that the stand is made from a bus stop.*

Mick   . . . you already gave me one.

Shay   Can't you take the two and breed them? You're never bleeding happy.

As **Shay** *talks,* **Bosco**, **Pascal** *and* **Ollie** *crowd through the door behind him.*

Bosco   What? A poker session is it? Great stuff.

Bosco *grabs the deck of cards on the beside table and begins to shuffle them.* **Ollie** *kneels beside the stereo and begins to pull CDs out all over the floor while* **Pascal** *wanders past* **Siobhan** *to root for food in the presses above the sink.*

Pascal (*nodding to* **Siobhan**)   How's it goin'? Bucking bad dose of the munchies.

He finds a packet of digestive biscuits and starts to wolf them.

Shay (*referring to* **Bosco** *as he lets the bus stop rest against the wall*)   Don't let him deal. We'll be here all night.

Shay *pulls up a chair.*

Bosco (*protesting*)   Ah now, house rules, dealer's choice.

Mick   Lads! (*Louder.*) Lads!

They stop and look at him.

Shay   All right, Bosco can deal, but play something we can open with. Any of them mushrooms left from last night, Mick? It's no wonder them old monks were mad bastards seeing visions. (*He looks at* **Mick** *who's trying to communicate with him.*) What?

Mick *indicates* **Siobhan**.

Shay   Oh yeah. (*He does a quick headcount.*) No, it's okay, we can deal with six off the one deck. Just reshuffle the shite.

Mick (*abandoning hope in sign language*)   Out lads!

Shay (*catching on*)   Oh yeah. Right.

He picks up the bus stop as he exits, followed by **Ollie** *with loose CDs under his arm and* **Pascal** *still clutching the biscuits. When they're gone* **Bosco** *looks up.*

Bosco   A round of In-Betweenies to deal?

He looks around at the empty bed-sit in surprise.

Mick (*firmly*)   Good night Bosco.

Bosco *exits, finally catching on.* **Mick** *closes the door, then looks at* **Siobhan**. *The jokey intimacy between them is broken.*

Siobhan   Expecting anyone else before I go?

Mick   What's your hurry?

Siobhan   Listen, it's late . . . sure, I'll see you again some time.

Mick (*appealing with a half-shrug*)   Okay, so I don't own a car.

Siobhan (*smiles*)   I never cared if you did. You were on my way home.

Mick (*glancing at the floor*)   It's a pretty classy Dinky, mind you. It shows character.

Siobhan (*laughs*)   It shows neck. (*Uncertain pause.*) I better go . . . it's late.

Mick (*producing a bottle of brandy from his pocket*)   Go on, have one drink anyway . . . before you go.

Siobhan *takes a slug and hands it back to him, as she rises to her feet.* **Mick** *stares at her as she brushes her clothes down, then scans the ceiling wistfully.* **Siobhan** *looks at him.*

Siobhan   Are you all right?

Mick   Ah yeah. I was just . . . thinking.

Siobhan   What?

Mick   If pigs could fly.

Siobhan (*puzzled*)   What?

Mick (*tentatively, with an impish grin*)   You wouldn't *really* want to go home.

Siobhan *scans the ceiling as well as if studiously examining something.*

Siobhan   Well . . . maybe I don't (*Pause.*) just yet. Back seats bore me anyway.

Mick   This one has a special feature.

He lifts the Dinky car up and hands it to her, pointing to the driver's door. **Siobhan** *opens it and then prises something out with her finger. She holds up a small plastic bag.*

Mick   Of course it's a small model, but I've taken some nice trips in it.

Siobhan   The last of the famous mushrooms.

Mick (*pointing at a battered television, balanced precariously on a mound of books*)   The only way to get colour on that set. Try some.

Siobhan *looks around the flat, then up at the bare light bulb.*

Siobhan (*suggestively*)   They'd taste nicer after dark.

Mick *grins and hands her the brandy.* **Siobhan** *swallows a couple of stringy mushrooms as* **Mick** *switches off the light, plunging the stage into darkness. We hear him staggering slightly as he begins to grope around the bed-sit for her.*

Mick   Siobhan? (*More worried.*) Siobhan? Ah now don't go asleep on me. Sio . . .

He gives a startled shout as **Siobhan** *suddenly lunges onto his back.*

Siobhan (*mock Oriental accent*)   Kato!

Mick   Good Jaysus, ahhh . . .

There is the creak of springs as they land on the bed.

Mick   Never spilt a drop. My God, you're a woman with class.

Siobhan   Have you glasses?

Mick   Why, have you germs?

There is the noise of drinking.

Siobhan (*giggles*)   Wait, you're spilling it on me.

Mick   Don't worry, I'll lick it off.

We hear the rustle of clothes and sounds of heavy breathing as 'Captain Beaky' begins to play in **Bosco**'s *flat, adding to the chorus of background noise.*

Siobhan   The music, can you not kill the music?

There is a click as **Mick** *turns on the bedside lamp.* **Siobhan** *and himself are beneath the sheets.*

Mick   No, but I can drown it.

He climbs out of bed in his underpants, flicks on his stereo, turns off the light again and dives back into bed as the stage is filled with the swelling chorus of 'They Got Elvis on a UFO' as if sung by strangulated ducks on speed while **Mick** *and* **Siobhan** *moan.*

Scene Two

Night gives way to morning as lights rise to suggest the sun battling through the pulled curtains. A bird twitters outside the window. The empty brandy bottle lies on the floor near the bed. **Mick** *gradually raises his head as though it were a painful and delicate operation. A look of shock crosses his face when he discovers the body beside him. His head sinks back onto the pillow. The movement wakes* **Siobhan** *who tries to focus her eyes on the unfamiliar room, then sits up with a jerk and stares down at* **Mick** *before her head also sinks back. After a moment she cuddles against him.*

Siobhan (*affectionate but slightly awkward, unsure of what response she will receive*) Am I still your cuddly toy? (**Mick** *groans faintly.*) Is my voice still sweeter than Christy O'Connor Jr playing the spoons?

Mick (*weakly*) Oh God.

Siobhan Still you were great all the same, Lance.

Mick My name's Mick. I told you I had a lance.

Siobhan Only teasing. (*More seriously.*) Listen Mick, I'll be late for work. Have you any food in the gaff? (**Mick** *moans piteously.*) What's wrong?

Mick My life's passing before my eyes. I hate repeats.

Siobhan Food. What do you have for breakfast?

Mick (*sighs*) A cigarette, a shite and a good look around.

Siobhan Be serious.

Mick (*pulling himself together*) Sorry, I generally dine out.

I'm a bit disorganised.

Siobhan (*looking around*)   And the seven dwarfs were a bit short. Here, I've got to go to work.

She begins putting on items of underclothing in bed, then wiggles out to get quickly into her dress. It is very obviously a fairly daring night-time outfit.

Mick   In that?

Siobhan (*smiles*)   I had only gone out for a pint of milk.

Mick   Those are the dangerous times.

There is an awkward silence with neither knowing what to say.

Mick (*tentatively*)   Siobhan?

Siobhan (*hopefully*)   Yes Mick.

Mick   Could I ask you a very great favour?

Siobhan (*pause*)   You know you don't have to.

Mick   No ... I want to.

Siobhan (*coyly*)   Ask away then.

Mick   You wouldn't phone in sick for me?

Siobhan's *disappointment is visible, but she says nothing.*

Mick   The Mobile Libraries. The number's on the wall beside the hall phone.

Siobhan   What will I tell them?

Mick (*thinks*)   *Playschool*'s on television.

Siobhan   You enjoy *Playschool*?

Mick (*sighs*)   It certainly beats work.

Siobhan   I've got to tell them something.

Mick *tries to think of an excuse but too many brain cells have been lost in the night.*

Mick (*weakly*)   You could tell them I've taken to the bed.

Siobhan (*sighs*)   Leave it to me. Michael. . . ?

Mick   Flaherty. Miss Siobhan. . . ?

Siobhan (*indignant*)   Mrs! (*Smiles.*) Ms Connolly.

She exits, leaving the flat door open. **Mick** *holds his head carefully in both hands. We hear her dialling and her indistinct voice phoning in sick for him. There is the sound of heavy footsteps in the hall and of a door opening.*

Shay (*offstage, with a laugh*)   Morning Bosco! Any more of the Drogheda boat people arrive in the meantime?

Bosco (*offstage*)   That's not funny you know. (*Quieter, in reply to muffled sounds behind him.*) What? He said nothing lads, never mind him.

Shay *enters* **Mick***'s bed-sit indignantly, holding an envelope in his outstretched hand. He walks straight across the bed to glance through the curtains suspiciously, as* **Mick** *looks up wearily at him.*

Shay   Is she gone? I hope you scored better than I did at the poker. (*He turns to thrust the letter at* **Mick** *in the bed.*) Okay, so tell me I'm imagining it this time. What's that?

He points towards the back of the envelope. **Mick** *takes it from him as* **Shay** *returns to the window to survey the street outside suspiciously.*

Mick   Ever learn to knock, Shay? (*He examines the envelope.*) It's a quarter-inch gap where your dear mother ran out of lip. What's it doing outside?

Shay (*turning*)   Pissing rain. It's been opened. It's obvious. A fool could see it. Any mushrooms left?

Mick (*handing the letter back to him*)   My granny. Listen Shay, I don't know how to break this to you.

Shay (*worried*)   What? Have you seen someone? I *knew* your man wasn't sheltering from the rain at that bus stop across the road last week.

Mick (*slowly as if to a foreigner with little English*)   Nobody is opening your mail. Nobody is tapping the telephone. Nobody is watching the house. The great wide world out there doesn't know who you are and it doesn't give a shite.

Shay (*snatching the letter back indignantly*)   You just watch who you're calling a nonentity, right!

Shay storms out, meeting **Siobhan** *on her way in.*

Shay (*looking at* **Siobhan**'s *outfit*)   Come on, ye divil, ye!

Siobhan (*coldly*)   Go on yourself. Slap it up on the table and we'll see what you're made of. (*She turns to* **Mick** *as* **Shay** *exits.*) Who's your friend?

Mick   The Mata Hari of Mountmellick.

Siobhan   I believe you. (*Briskly, reaching for her coat.*) It's a bit of a waste, isn't it?

Mick   What?

Siobhan   Having doors around here. Anyway, you're in business.

Mick (*snuggling down in the bed*)   Thanks.

Siobhan   How do you feel?

Mick   Like the song said, My head hurts, my feet stink and I don't love Jesus.

Siobhan (*turning to leave*)   I doubt if you love anything.

Mick   That's not fair. I love St Martin, Patron Saint of Hopeless Causes.

Siobhan   St Jude is hopeless causes.

Mick   All foreign bodies look the same to me. Anyway, you wouldn't want to rely on the living when you follow

Shelbourne Football Club.

Siobhan (*pausing at the door in surprise*)   Shelbourne?
Good God, you are a romantic. Ben Hannigan?

Mick (*lifting himself up on one elbow in surprise*)   Ben
Hannigan? What do you know about Ben Hannigan?

Siobhan   Eric Barber. Paddy Roche. (*Deliberately fumbles,
then drops her bag.*) The safest pair of hands since the
Venus de Milo!

Mick (*stunned*)   You weren't even born when they played.

Siobhan   It was half-price admission for embryos. I
almost didn't come out when I smelt the watery Bovril.

Mick   The smell of my childhood, Tolka Park. Surely I
must have seen you there?

Siobhan   My da used to take me to the terraces.
They reminded him of his country childhood, acres of
open spaces and you'd never meet a soul.

Mick   My God, you were that blob at the far end of
the ground. I always thought it was a seagull with a
broken wing.

Siobhan   My brothers used to bar me from the
twenty-questions sessions. I had to bribe my way back in
with cigarettes.

Mick (*thinks*)   Who played eleven minutes on his debut
for Ireland and scored an equaliser away from home?

Siobhan   Joe Waters of course. Turkey.

Mick   Are you a vision or real?

Siobhan   What's the smallest country ever to field a
team in a European club championship match?

Mick   What? Wait . . . (*He lifts the blankets and looks
down.*) I'm not dressed, it's not fair. (*He thinks.*) Andorra?

Siobhan   Liechtenstein.

Mick (*winces*) Don't mention Liechtenstein! I'd bar you from my shed as well. (*Pause.*) Siobhan?

Siobhan What?

Mick Can I ask you a really, really great favour?

Siobhan I don't make breakfast.

Mick No, seriously. Listen I'm no good at this sort of thing. You're not seeing me at my best here. Like, I've wanted to ask you since I woke up, but I just . . . well, couldn't get a way around to it. (*Pause.*) Can I see you again?

Siobhan You don't have to.

Mick I want to.

Siobhan Maybe.

Mick Please. Pretty please.

Siobhan (*smiles*) Okay.

Mick Tomorrow night?

Siobhan Tomorrow night.

Mick George's Street?

Siobhan Where?

Mick The glass shelter at the 16 bus stop.

Siobhan Why? Where are we going?

Mick Harold's Cross dog track, of course. I mean it is a Thursday.

Siobhan Don't wait after midnight if I'm not there.

Mick If you don't come I promise to throw myself in front of the mechanical hare. It will be on your conscience that I was savaged by muzzled greyhounds!

Mick grins and she blows him a kiss as she is about to close the door. Behind her there is a sudden evacuation of bodies from

Bosco's *flat.*

Bosco (*offstage*)   Cheers lads.

Siobhan *is forced back into the room followed by* **Pascal**.

Pascal (*to* **Siobhan**)   Still here? Well, how did yous make out together, so?

Ollie (*offstage*)   See you next week, Bosco.

Ollie *appears in the doorway ready to pull* **Pascal** *back out into the corridor.*

Ollie   Will you come on, Pascal. You'll be interrupting all class of tears and recriminations. (*He looks towards the window.*) That's not rain, is it? It's a tad wet. Sure, will we go home at all?

Bosco (*anxiously, offstage*)   Ah now, it's only a shower, lads.

Pascal (*staring at the window*)   Ah, buck it . . . bucking oul rain bucking down.

Siobhan *stares at* **Pascal** *mumbling to himself, almost in a world of his own.*

Ollie   Ah don't mind him miss, a tad inarticulate in the mornings.

Pascal (*glaring at* **Ollie**)   Buck off you, I am not. I never bucking wet the bucking bed yet.

Siobhan *steps back as the two lads vanish down the hall. The front door slams and she looks at* **Mick**.

Siobhan (*unsure if she heard right*)   Bucking?

Mick   Pascal's ma made him swear on Saint Oliver Plunkett's head that a curse would never pass his lips.

Siobhan   Get away.

Mick   That's the Dublin branch of the Drogheda United Supporters Club next door.

Siobhan (*sneaking a glance across*)   No wonder the room's so small.

She goes to exit again.

Mick   One last thing.

Siobhan (*stops*)   What?

Mick   Eh, you wouldn't just fill the kettle while you're there?

Siobhan   How do you get to be so lazy?

Mick   Hard work and practice.

She quickly fills the kettle beside her, switches it on and heads for the door.

Siobhan   Goodbye, Mick.

Siobhan *exits, closing the door.* **Mick** *waits a moment then throws his fist in the air in celebration before suddenly grimacing and holding his head again.*

Mick   Love. It must be love. (*He thinks, then shouts after her.*) Siobhan? Do you play snooker? (*No reply. He talks to himself quietly.*) There must be a catch: her mother's a Fianna Fail councillor, her father sleeps with the Bishop of Clonfert. Nobody can be that nice. (*He raises a hand to his head.*) Gentle does it. Lie there and relax. Dangerous to get up too quickly on a Wednesday.

He lies back, then rises on one elbow to reach for his trousers on the floor. He raids each pocket and loose change rains from them until, from the pile of coins on the bed, he picks up and unfurls a crumpled five-pound note

A note? On a Wednesday? A beggar must have given it to me.

He continues searching his pockets and finally an equally crumpled packet of cigarettes is discovered. He lights one and is lost in a violent fit of coughing.

That's better. (*Pause.*) Liechtenstein?

He searches the bedclothes and discovers a small piece of silver foil.

Thanks be to God for lust. There's still some dope left.

He rises on one elbow to reach for a sweeping brush under the bed. He uses it to knock over a small pile of books on the floor and sweeps four hardback volumes across the floor towards him. He bends down to pick them up.

(*Examining the books.*) Who have we got this morning? Caesar's *Gallic Wars* in Latin; Arthur Schopenhauer, he's the boy to put manners on you during a peaceful morning in bed; *Winnie-the-Pooh*, we could live with that; Churchill's *History of the Second World War, Volume Six* – Jaysus, if that one wasn't stolen I'd bring it back. No, definitely Schopenhauer, there's too much sex and violence in the others for a Wednesday. (*Mock radio presenter's voice.*) But first, a word from our sponsors.

Mick *briefly looks up, hearing footsteps in the hall and a knocking on* **Bosco**'s *door, as he opens a packet of cigarette papers, sticks two together on top of the book, breaks open a cigarette and empties half the tobacco onto the skins before opening the silver foil. He begins to crumple the hash carefully over the tobacco, then searches his pockets and looks around.*

Mick   Roach paper. Never any shagging roach paper. (*He looks at the books.*) Shag this intellectual snobbery, will I never remember to steal some softbacks in work for a change?

There are three sudden knocks on his own door. He looks round in alarm, carefully picks up the book with the half-rolled joint on it, rises from the bed reluctantly and is about to put it under the bed when, simultaneously, the knocking reoccurs and he is seized by another fit of coughing which scatters the contents of the cigarette papers over the floor.

Mick   All right, I'm coming.

He gets into his jeans and opens the door cautiously.

Elder Osborne (*offstage in a strong American accent*) Very sorry to trouble you sir. We're just doing a survey and we were wondering if you would mind answering a few questions?

Mick (*stepping back slightly so that we can see **Elder Osborne** and **Elder Stanford***) Eh . . . no offence like but I'm very busy just now . . .

Elder Osborne It won't take a moment.

Mick And I'm skint.

Elder Osborne (*hurt voice*) We're not salesmen.

Mick (*peering at them again*) Oh, sorry. Jehovah's Witnesses?

Elder Osborne (*even more offended*) We are from the Church of Latter-Day Saints of Jesus Christ! (**Mick** *looks blank.*) Mormons.

Mick I know how you feel lads, somebody called me a Bohs fan once. Actually I'm not really religious. So nothing personal, but . . .

Elder Osborne Oh good! You're the very person we want to talk to so.

Mick I am? (*Pause.*) How did you get in, boys?

Elder Stanford The front door was open to receive us.

Mick I'll strangle that Bosco. Listen, I've a very sore head, lads.

Elder Osborne Well the fact is Mr. . . ?

Mick Mick.

Elder Osborne The fact is, Michael, that we could have finished the survey in the time we've been discussing this.

Mick   How many doors have you knocked on this morning?

Elder Osborne   Nobody ever said the work of the Lord was easy. 'In the desert prepare / The way for the Lord / Make straight in the wilderness / A highway for the Lord.' Isaiah 40:3.

Mick   'Anyone who'se been turned down / Is bound to be a friend of mine.' John Prine. And I suppose it is raining. I haven't the strength to argue. Five minutes though to get dry and that's it.

He steps back and the two **Mormons** *eagerly enter the bed-sit. They are young, perfectly dressed with glasses and very sincere.* **Elder Osborne** *is the more senior of them and inclined to take the lead.* **Elder Stanford** *is inclined to follow the textbook in everything but increasingly as the play progresses he oversteps the mark, annoying* **Elder Osborne**. *They survey the room with a look of vague disbelief. The kettle is boiling and* **Mick** *goes over to it. He selects the least dirty cup, tosses in a tea bag and fills it up. In this scene* **Mick** *is as much amused as bewildered by his visitors.*

Mick   Eh tea? (**Elder Osborne** *coughs and they both shake their heads.*) Sorry. Eh . . . coffee? Jaysus that's worse.

Elder Osborne   Hot water. Thank you.

Mick   Oh yeah.

He rinses two more cups, fills them with hot water and brings them over to the two chairs when the **Mormons** *have sat down. They smile, take them off him and each have a sip.*

Mick (*at a loss*)   Eh . . . is it strong enough?

Both smile and nod. **Mick** *sits on the edge of the bed with his tea. There is silence as the visitors look around.*

Elder Osborne   Nice place.

Mick   Thanks.

Elder Stanford   God groweth even in the wilderness.

Elder Stanford *smiles across at his companion. Having gained entry they now seem content to sit in silence.*

Mick (*cautiously*) It was just a couple of questions wasn't it? (*They smile in reply.*) Do you . . . eh . . . think you could ask them?

Elder Stanford We will.

Yet they continue looking around them.

Mick (*hopefully*) Soon?

Elder Stanford In time.

Elder Osborne Often when people turn us away I think it is not to us they are refusing to open their doors but to themselves, not us they are afraid of but their own souls. Are you frightened of us, Michael, or of your spiritual self?

Mick Religion's a dangerous business lads. Why not just take the weight off your feet and enjoy the hot water?

Elder Osborne What possible harm could it do you?

Mick Look at Cyril Knowles' brother. Gave up playing for Wolves that season they could have won the Cup.

Elder Osborne Flippancy is the weapon those who are hurt always hide behind. You were not busy this morning when we called, Michael. (*He nods towards the bed.*) You were still lying there.

Mick It's only half-nine boys.

Elder Stanford (*butts in*) This is what they call 'the front line' in training. Fine able-bodied creatures like you cast off on the scrap heap of society, itching to work if you could only find a job.

Mick *starts to grin, amused at the conversation.*

Elder Osborne I feel for you, Michael, in your

helplessness. (*He leans forward.*) What were your thoughts this morning as you rose from your lonely bed?

Mick Well eh ... (*Mumbles.*) it was a bit crowded actually.

Elder Osborne Could you have known friends were so close at hand? That Elder Stanford and I were walking these streets at that very moment?

Elder Stanford (*leaning forward also*) Knocking on doors, searching for the right one. It is the black sheep the good shepherd will look for. Is that right, Elder Osborne?

Mick (*at a loss*) I was never much into sheep myself. Saw this film once in Holland, but ... eh ... never mind.

Elder Stanford You were crying in the wilderness, thinking no one could hear and yet He hears everything. We have found you in time to lift you from this squalor, this degradation ...

Mick Ah hold on now. I was going to clean it up.

Elder Stanford ... to lead you back to the light of God.

Mick I don't want to be rude boys, but you're barking up the wrong tree.

Elder Osborne Doubts are natural. We will answer all your questions in time.

Mick Is this all in the questionnaire?

Elder Osborne We don't need a questionnaire, Michael, to see the way you are, to feel your despair without a job or a future, with nobody to share your burden. Michael, we have come to share your burden. To tell you it is not your fault. We know how you are suppressed with your socialist newspapers and your left-wing governments, your communist health service and newscasters taking their orders from Moscow. And you are their helpless victim, forced out of work by their unemployment incentive, stripped of your freedom by their rent allowances.

Mick   Merciful hour. The magic mushrooms weren't in it.

Elder Osborne   We know your shame, but we have come here to talk of joy, to lead you out into the light. Michael, I want to leave you this book. I know you have a thousand questions to ask, a thousand barriers to break down that you have built around your true self. Those questions will all be answered in time. (*He reaches into his briefcase.*) Read this book for now.

Mick   Whatever you're on it's great stuff lads, but your five minutes is up.

Elder Osborne *produces a hardback volume which he holds out to* **Mick**.

Listen lads, I've just got this aversion to joining anything, and I've a lot of reading of my own to get through. No disrespect but . . . (*A new note enters his voice as he looks at the book.*) eh . . . you don't have one with a cardboard cover, do you?

The **Mormons** *smile at each other.*

Elder Stanford   Humility is the first sign of repentance.

Elder Osborne   Take this one, Michael. You deserve the best.

Mick (*humbly*)   No, I couldn't.

He hands it back to **Elder Stanford** *who produces a softbound edition which he places in* **Mick**'s *hands.*

Elder Osborne   I am touched, Michael, by your humility.

Mick (*raising a hand modestly*)   No, say nothing. Please.
But if you don't mind, I . . . eh . . . have some thinking
to do.

Elder Osborne   Of course, Michael. Goodbye for
now. (*To* **Elder Stanford**.) A sign, Elder Stanford, after
all our walking.

Mick *shows them to the door, shakes their hands and closes the
door after them. He lies against it in relief, then looks down at the
book in his hand, examines the cover carefully before tearing a
small strip off it. He rolls the cardboard expertly between his
fingers, then looks up.*

Mick (*delighted*)   Bleeding great roach paper!

*Suddenly below him 'Paper Roses' sung by Maisie McDaniel
starts to play in the basement flat. He looks down and frowns as
the stage goes dark.*

Scene Three

*The music fades. The lights go up again, lit for evening. The bed-
sit looks the same, except that the book* **Mick** *was given is
displayed on the bedside locker, with most of its front cover gone.*
Mick *enters, leaving the door open, and after a quick look
through the curtains, exits again to return with two estate agent's
signs, one large and the other small. He throws them down near
the fireplace, into which he throws a half-packet of firelighters and,
taking up an axe, begins to chop up the smaller sign and pile the
pieces into the grate. There is a knocking on the closed door and*
Mick *looks around in panic as if searching for a way out.*

Mick (*quietly, looking towards heaven*)   Not again Lord.
(*Louder.*) Who is it?

Bosco (*offstage*)   Are those bastards from Drogheda
around Mick? Is it safe?

Mick *looks visibly relieved as he opens the door. Although dressed
in scruffy jeans and a dirty tee-shirt* **Bosco** *is actually older*

than **Mick**. *He has a look of perpetual adolescence and the pallor of creatures rarely exposed to daylight. He enters with both hands locked together as if in prayer and his eyes fixed on the small hole formed by the thumb of his left hand and index finger of his right.*

Mick The wetbacks haven't arrived tonight. They must have stepped up patrols on the Louth border.

Bosco The shaggers have my life destroyed. Even the provincial bus driver is starting to stop outside the front door. Ever since Ollie's da died and he inherited the disability pass.

Mick You know your bed-sit isn't exactly Venice in springtime.

Bosco Beats shagging Drogheda on the dole. Oh, I can't blame the lads. You get up in the morning, walk down the town, into the cathedral for a gawk at Oliver Plunkett's head, home for dinner, back down, another gander at the head, walk round in the pissings of rain, back in for a last look at the head. All there has been to do in Drogheda for the last three hundred years is look at the head of Saint Oliver Plunkett.

Mick *has resumed chopping up the sign at the fireplace.*

Mick When are they due?

Bosco Today or tomorrow. They've got to get the dole for their brothers who are over in Boston on the black.

Mick Why can't they collect it in Drogheda?

Bosco Sure they've to collect it for themselves up there.

Mick *notices* **Bosco***'s hands and nods towards them.*

Mick Wanker's cramp, is it?

Bosco (*looking down and remembering*) Oh yeah. Any Blu-Tack Mick?

Mick   Somewhere.

Bosco   Find it quick, my hands are killing me.

Mick *removes a poster from the wall and rolls up the four bits of Blu-Tack from the back of it.*

Bosco   Stick it in there, go on.

Mick *presses the Blu-Tack into the valley between* **Bosco***'s hands and when it is wedged there* **Bosco** *finally releases them and stares at the lump of Blu-Tack in his palm.*

Bosco   You're a mate. Com'ere, (*He looks around.*) is it cool to roll?

Mick   Yeah, sure.

Bosco   Oh great. (*Stops and thinks.*) Have you any dope?

Mick (*sighs*)   In my jacket pocket.

Bosco   Fair play to you. (*He goes to pick up* **Mick***'s jacket, then stops to show* **Mick** *the Blu-Tack.*) So, what ya think?

Mick   Very nice Blu-Tack. Good vintage I'm sure.

Bosco   No, the size of it? (**Mick** *still has no idea what the conversation is about.*) For thirty spots, what do ya think?

Mick   What are you on about, Bosco?

Bosco   I met this mot in a pub, and she offered it to me. Won't have it till Friday but it's a thirty-spot deal. Moroccan Black. I made a hole in my hands (*He joins them together again.*) and I said to her Is it that size, or this size and she said it was this size. (*He holds up the Blu-Tack.*) So what you think? Thirty spots? Did I do well?

Mick   You paid her cash?

There is a sudden knocking on the door and **Bosco** *throws the Blu-Tack away from him onto the chair.*

Bosco (*alarmed*) The Drug Squad! How they find out so fast?

Mick You're okay, Blu-Tack isn't proscribed yet. (*Calls politely.*) Who is it?

Elder Osborne (*offstage*) Glad we caught you in again, Michael.

Mick Why me Lord? Why me?

Quickly **Mick** *opens the locker and takes out empty bottles of spirits and wine to pile up on the table. He grabs the jar of coffee and the tea bags to display prominently, lights three cigarettes, puts one of them smoking in the ashtray, one between his lips and the third in* **Bosco**'s *surprised mouth.*

Bosco Oh cheers, you're a mate. What is it, another poker session? I'm skint after that one last night. We didn't get out of here until dawn.

Mick Only two rules for a life of contemplation and retreat, Bosco. Never leave the bed on a Wednesday unless you really have to and never ever run short of roach paper.

Mick *is about to answer the knock when he spies the book with the cover almost gone. He puts it under the mattress, then opens the door.*

(*Wearily.*) The third time this week, lads. Is there nobody else to save in Dublin?

Elder Osborne You're looking a new man already, Michael.

The **Mormons** *walk past him and take the same seats, smiling at first, although taken aback by the display on the table.* **Bosco** *has been rooting in* **Mick**'s *jacket and finds the scrap of tin foil. He turns and looks at the* **Mormons**.

Bosco Howya lads. Com'ere, is it cool to roll? (*He suddenly darts forward.*) Get up ye bastard, you're sitting on my Blu-Tack!

They jump up in alarm to look behind them and **Elder Stanford** *prises it from the seat of his trousers. He hands it to* **Bosco**, *who takes it dejectedly, trying to mould it back into the size it had been.*

Mick (*nodding towards the door*) Bosco.

Bosco Oh yeah. Nice to meet you lads. I'll see yous again. (*He is almost at the door when he cannot resist turning back to them. He produces the Blu-Tack.*) Be honest lads, what do you think? Thirty spots. Did I do well? Did I?

Elder Stanford (*confused*) Well, eh, I'm sure you did. Where did you get it?

Bosco That would be telling, eh. But Shay now upstairs is the man you boys should see.

Elder Stanford (*eagerly*) Shay. Oh, we will certainly give him a call. And maybe yourself?

Bosco (*modestly*) Ah no, Shay is big time, get you anything you want. But I can leave you some of this when I get it.

Elder Osborne Thanks anyway, we have thumb tacks.

Bosco (*stunned*) Jaysus, what do you do with those?

Mick *half-lifts* **Bosco** *towards the door as the two* **Mormons** *stare blankly at him.* **Mick** *closes the door.*

Elder Osborne Nice lad.

Elder Stanford Likes sticking things.

Mick He does.

Elder Stanford Very helpful too about the poor lad upstairs. We will certainly call to comfort him.

Mick I really wouldn't do that. For your own safety.

Elder Stanford (*looking around*) Had you eh . . . a party last night?

Mick No, no. Just myself (*He pulls on his cigarette as he tries to put conviction into his voice.*) and, eh . . . a few women you know. But, I won't tell you any more because you'd see you're wasting your time.

Elder Osborne No Michael, you can be honest with us.

Mick Ah no lads, you've been very good to call in every second night and I'd hate to disillusion you. (*He pauses, but neither* **Mormon** *replies.*) Well, if you insist. They were sisters, you see . . . the three of them . . . from the West of Ireland. Very poor families there, all the children sleep in the one bed. I suppose they'd just never got out of the habit. Though of course with so much drugs and alcohol and caffeine and tobacco I don't remember much about it. It all got very confusing about who was feeling who. But then you're men of the world. You know the score yourselves.

Elder Stanford (*wide-eyed*) Hardly.

Mick Anyway when the three of them had left . . . for school . . . and I lay here in the ashes of another night of lust, I started thinking that . . . well I'm not proud of the way I am, but I'm not ashamed of it either. I just guess that I'm not the saveable type. I'm sorry you boys have put in so much time and I really do appreciate it. But that's just the way it is. Don't be disheartened. There'll be others to save.

Elder Osborne Oh we're not in the least. In fact we're heartened. It is the black sheep that the good shepherd seeks. Your words only prove that God has given you to us to save. We know it will not be easy, Michael, brother . . .

Mick (*in despair*) Ah now, go easy lads.

Elder Osborne We are in this together. Your misery must be great for you to wallow so deeply in filth. But all the richer will be your salvation. I want you to know our footsteps will be with yours down every inch of that long road to repentance.

Mick (*dejected*)   Ah lads. Can't you see that I don't want repentance. All my life I just wanted to be left alone.

Elder Osborne   How do you really know what you want unless you listen to your soul? When I look at you I see a lost and frightened child, but one too stubborn to cry for help. You can neither hide nor run from yourself.

Elder Stanford   Ambition, Michael. You have to strive for something. What do you want from life?

Mick   I'd accept a written apology. I don't know how to break this to you but I'm actually very happy in my life. Okay, maybe one day I'll get to spend all my time reading half-cracked philosophers and watching Italian football from the bed. But it's not that bad as it is.

Elder Osborne   How far are you with the first book?

Mick   I haven't started the back cover yet.

Elder Osborne (*opening his case*)   Always the jokes, Michael. We'll leave you this one as well and a few magazines to pass around your friends.

Mick (*desperately searching for straws*)   If I brought back all the library books, would that not be enough repentance for now?

Elder Osborne   You only need one book, Michael. (*He leaves the pile of magazines and pamphlets down.*) Spread the good word, that's what we are all here for.

Mick (*anxious to get them out the door*)   Even if I'm not finding Our Lord with you lads, I'm certainly starting to mention him a lot. (*He opens the door.*) Now remember I may not be in much these evenings. Busy social life, especially with the Galway triplets . . . and their younger sister.

Elder Stanford Don't worry. We'll find you, Michael.

Mick *throws his eyes up to heaven as they exit. He closes the door and heads straight for the bed to climb in. There is a thunderous knocking on the door, which he ignores as he reaches for a book. The knock comes even louder and* **Mick** *rises reluctantly to open the door an inch and then fully.*

Mick (*disguising his alarm*) Ah, Mr Lewis, is it yourself? About the rent, I just seem to keep missing you these last weeks. Will you be around the same time on Friday?

Mick *steps back to allow the landlord to enter, still in the bottom-half of his police uniform.*

Mr Lewis (*West of Ireland accent*) Ah 'tis'nt the rent at all, though I will be around on Friday. No 'tis about your visitors. They seem fierce fond of you boy, fierce fond indeed. Oh I know, Mickey, I was your age once. 'Tis an age when the oul doubt begins to creep in, especially for a young country lad like yourself cut off from your family and your native place.

Mick I keep telling you, Mr Lewis, I'm actually from Fairview.

Mr Lewis (*unheeding*) Sure wasn't I in a same boat myself in this city forty years ago when I got my first posting in the guards. The oul doubt is a fierce man. 'Twould make you susceptible to alien influences, be it the drink (*Looks at the table.*) or the wee-men (*Looks at the bed.*) or them foreign fuddy-duddy religions. No, say nothing. Sure we're all mortal. But 'tis quare company for a young lad like you to be keeping, so I'll fix it to have two friends of mine, mature people from the Legion of Mary, over here tomorrow evening to drive all that foreign nonsense out. You'll thank me for this yet, Mickey. We'll have a good laugh about it one day.

Mick (*horrified*) No, honestly, Mr Lewis. It's very good of you but there's no need. I'm doing everything in my power to stop them calling.

Mr Lewis   Don't try to hide it, Mickey. Sure we're all Irishmen together. 'Twould prey on me conscience if I were to see you lose the faith. They're two of the best the Legion have. Have no fear about that. We'll have you a new man in days. (*He slaps* **Mick** *heartily on the back.*) God, you'll be climbing Croagh Patrick in your bare feet!

Mr Lewis *exits, leaving* **Mick** *horror-struck. He closes the door, walks slowly back to the bed and climbs into it as 'Ave Maria' by Dickie Rock starts in the flat below. He pulls the bedclothes over his face as the lights go down.*

Scene Four

In silhouette, moving in swift jerky motion as if in a speeded-up film, **Mick** *leaves the bed and opens the door to* **Mr Lewis** *who, with great backslapping, mimes introducing* **Mick** *to* **Lily** *and* **Jack**. **Mr Lewis** *exits and* **Lily** *and* **Jack** *sit on the sofa while* **Mick** *sinks back onto the edge of the bed. Music stops and the lights come up.* **Mick** *looks petrified at the couple before him still in their coats.*

Lily   You poor young fellow, caught in here like a rabbit in a trap. Sure how could you have known where to come for help?

Jack   Ah, we're always glad to help. Gets us out in the evenings too, nothing ever on that oul telly.

Lily   Lord, I envy you your youth. Oh the things we did, do you remember, Jack?

Jack (*looks puzzled*)   I think so.

Lily   But there's so many more temptations for young people now. If you saw the state of the young ones in O'Connell Street at night. Say what you like about that Boy George who used to swan around in dresses, but at least he covered his legs up! (*She hits* **Jack** *with her elbow for a response.*)

Jack Aye, he did that.

Lily A sound body and a sound mind, that's what I say. But sure, 'tisn't the women at all in your case Mr Lewis was telling us. 'Twould be better off if you were out at a few dances instead of sitting in here brooding.

Jack Or playing manly sports. Swinging a hurley is where you'd be safe from them Mormon buckos. (*He sneaks a look at* **Lily**.) There's great peace on the playing pitch.

Lily It only takes one crack in your armour for every Mormon and Jehovah to come nosing in. Before an innocent young gosoon like you knows it, they have you in up to your eyeballs, and you know the funny thing? (**Mick** *shakes his head, baffled.*) You wouldn't ever know you were doing wrong. Lack of information. I blame the schools for not teaching right from wrong. Sure you could be walking through a minefield and not know it. Now, child, are you familiar with the forbidden and suspect societies, especially the ones banned under pain of sin and excommunication?

Jack Aye, the Masons. 'The faithful must beware of associations which are secret, condemned, seditious, or suspect, or which seek to evade the legitimate vigilance of the Church.' Canon Law, No. 684. (*Pause.*) Can you get *Sky Sports* on that telly, son?

Lily 'Those who give their names to the Masonic sect incur by that very fact an excommunication which is reserved, in the simple manner, to the Holy See.' Canon Law, No. 2335.

Jack (*to* **Lily**) No, 'tis more likely he'd be involved in something with just a simple prohibition. Like the Independent Order Of Good Templars, the Odd-Fellows or the Knights of Pythias.

Lily Not to mention Spiritualist or Theosophical societies.

Jack The Friends of Israel Society.

Lily *and* **Jack** Or the Communist Party!

Lily Which only leaves the Societies Declared Suspect or Deserving of Caution like the Young Men's Christian Association, or Rotary clubs. You were never in a Rotary club were you?

Mick I was only ever in the Shelbourne Supporters Club.

Jack (*brightens up*) Wasn't Ben Hannigan a great oul player all the same. Before your time, but . . .

Lily Jack!

Jack Oh. I think you were safe enough there son.

Mick And I left that when I was eight. Honestly you can put your mind to rest, I've a life-long aversion to joining anything.

Lily Still the Mormons are the sly boys. Nosing in here brainwashing and you still wet behind the ears. (*Snorts.*) Polygamy how are you! Did they tell you the legend of the Golden Plates?

Mick Well, we hadn't really got beyond foreplay.

Lily Fabrication. More gold in a packet of Benson & Hedges. Coming in here looking for tolerance. Divil the bit they ever gave anyone themselves. If I had Brigham Young to myself for five minutes I'd grab him where the hair is short. Did they tell you about his speeches, 'Every spirit that confessed Joseph Smith is no prophet is of the Antichrist.' I'd give him the Antichrist. I suppose they were going to teach you to speak in tongues.

Mick I said I'd sooner stick to the Linguaphone.

There is a knock on the door. **Mick** *approaches it cautiously, opens it and stumbles back as* **Siobhan** *(in a short skirt) jumps in on him, wrapping her legs around his waist.*

Siobhan *(oriental roar)*   Kato! *(She slowly looks over* **Mick***'s shoulder and sees* **Lily** *and* **Jack** *transfixed by her entrance.)* Good Jaysus!

Mick *(to* **Jack***)*   Manly sports, was it?

Lily *(rising briskly)*   Well Jack, I think we've taken up enough of this young man's time for tonight.

Jack *(reluctantly)*   I suppose so.

Lily *sweeps towards the door with* **Jack** *in tow and exits.* **Jack** *pauses.*

Jack   Hello, miss. *(He looks back into the flat.)* It's great to get out in the evenings, son.

He exits and **Mick** *slowly lowers* **Siobhan** *to the ground.*

Siobhan   Sorry, Mick. I thought you were alone. Who was she?

Mick   Oh, my Aunt Ellen. Up for the Christmas shopping.

Siobhan   In August?

Mick   A fierce cautious woman. Let's get out of here before anybody else calls.

He grabs his jacket, kisses **Siobhan***, puts his arm around her, flicks the light switch to put the bed-sit into darkness and they exit. There is brief silence, then the sound of knocking.*

Mr Lewis *(offstage)*   Mickey, they're two of the best in the Legion. I'll be into you for that back rent on Friday.

There is silence again, followed by thunderous knocking.

Bosco *(offstage)*   Thirty spots, Mick. Be honest, was I robbed?

Scene Five

After a brief blackout, music comes faintly from downstairs as the door opens again and, in slowly flashing light, **Mick** *and* **Siobhan** *enter less drunkenly than on the first night. Initially we don't know where the light is coming from; then, as lights rise slightly, we realise that* **Mick** *has a stolen roadworks lamp under his jumper. He takes it out to look at it.*

Mick   What'll I do with the shagging thing?

He places it on the table and goes over to the locker while **Siobhan** *sits on the bed to remove a six-pack from a carrier bag. The lamp (along with some filled-in light) lights the rest of the scene.*

Mick (*rooting around*)   Jaysus, it's just like poker, I can never get an opener. Hang on, here's one.

He rises, holding the opener and opens two bottles from her lap, raising one to his lips.

Cheers!

He sits beside her on the bed and they drink, gazing at the flashing light.

Siobhan   Romantic, isn't it.

Mick   Yeah, like being at a rave in Cloghar Head.

Siobhan   When were you ever at a rave? You'd be too lazy to queue.

Mick   I'm not lazy, I'm just trying to live my life in my own way in the Independent Republic of Mickonia. It's hard enough being Monarch, Chancellor and Official Leader of the Opposition, but Minister for Defence is where my work is really cut out. Half the world is perpetually trying to annex me. Every Christmas my brother-in-laws take it as a personal insult that I don't own a car or haven't got promoted in work yet. They can't get it into their skulls that I've taken a solemn vow of apathy against their world.

Siobhan That's just an excuse to be a lazy bollocks.

Mick Listen, it's lazy people who get caught up in that madness out there – licking some arse for promotion, joining a building society to save for some house, voting for the Soldiers of Density, the Warriors of Cuchulainn or the Progressive Shan Bhean Phochters. I've stepped out of that world and you won't believe how much hard work and vigilance it takes to get people to simply leave me alone.

Siobhan Okay, not lazy then, but cynical.

Mick The Cynics were the finest philosophers in the ancient world. The name comes from the Greek for Dog, after old Diogenes of Sinope who founded them and was a bit of a dog himself. (**Mick** *briefly picks up the lamp.*) He used to go around in broad daylight with one of these lit up, trying to find an honest man. Old Diogenes thought we should live without possessions or artificial complications to bind us down, scornful of sexual restraint or social institutions, as free as the dogs in the street.

Siobhan That explains your sexual preferences, anyway.

Mick (*mock hurt*) Ah now. Diogenes is the patron saint of Mickonia.

Siobhan (*gentle teasing*) Him and Peter Pan. You're gas, you've never grown up, Mick? Was that woman really your aunt?

Mick Sure, wouldn't I be too lazy to invent a lie? (*He puts his arm around her.*) Come here to me and less of this oul chat.

Siobhan I could get fond of you, you know that.

Mick (*as serious as he can get*) Diogenes himself would make room for you in his tub.

He kisses **Siobhan** *who pushes him away slightly.*

Siobhan   That light. I feel like I'm on a building site.

Mick *picks up the lantern and looks around, unable to kill its light. He opens the wardrobe, sticks it inside and closes the door, putting the stage into almost total darkness.*

Mick (*darkly*)   Okay Kato. Lesson No. 157.

We hear **Siobhan** *giggle as* **Mick** *jumps onto the bed. There is a pause to suggest time passing before some more light bleeds in.*

Siobhan (*sleepily*)   Mick? (*He mutters in his sleep.*) Wake up Mick, I have to go.

Mick (*sleepily*)   Phone in sick for me.

Siobhan   Mick, wake up and put the light on. I told you I can't stay the night. Where are my clothes? Can you find my panties? It was you threw them away.

Mick   Threw them away? I thought I ate them.

He switches on the bedside lamp and begins to root around on one side of the floor nearest the audience while **Siobhan** *searches the top of the bed. He finds her panties and holds them up, about to call her, before suddenly changing his mind and stuffing them down into his own underpants.*

Siobhan (*pulling on her dress under the blankets*)   Shag it, I'll go without them. I'll get a taxi at the rank easily enough, won't I? I suppose there's no chance of an escort?

Mick   People would think we were walking out.

Siobhan   If I'm murdered I'll come back and haunt you. Give us a kiss then.

They kiss and **Mick** *gets out of bed to see her to the door.*

Siobhan   Friday night then, dog. Turn up drunk and I'll kill you.

Mick   Turn up sober and I'll kill you.

He closes the door after her and turns to thoughtfully consider her panties which he removes from his underpants. He climbs back into bed and switches out the light.

Scene Six

The sound of music begins, being played by **Mick**. *After a moment we hear knocking and the lights come up.* **Mick** *stands on the bed, holding a pitching wedge. There is a small pile of table-tennis balls at his feet and a waste bin near the door with more clustered around it. He takes the cigarette from his mouth.*

Mick   Mondays, Wednesdays and Fridays the Mormons. Tuesdays and Thursdays the Legion of Mary. (*He thinks.*) Friday, it has to be the Church of Jesus Christ of Latter-Day Saints. (*Shouts.*) Is that you lads?

Elder Osborne (*offstage*)   Nice to hear you in, Michael.

When **Mick** *hears* **Elder Osborne***'s voice he jumps from the bed, turns off the music and begins to remove all his clothes until he is only wearing the panties which* **Siobhan** *had lost in the last scene. He takes a bag from under the bed and produces from it a bra which he fits clumsily on. He looks around, then stuffs two table-tennis balls into the bra before approaching the door. He furtively blesses himself, looks heavenwards and gives a little thumbs up sign.*

Mick   It's going to be a shock lads but I can't hide it any longer. You're going to have to see me as I am, a wretched, pathetic creature. (*He opens the door. The* **Mormons** *enter and stand in shock.*) I know. I hate to disappoint you, but I can't help myself. Now can't you see that I'm just not convertible? I mean ask yourself, am I really Mormon material?

Elder Osborne (*shocked*)   We know you were bad, Michael, but really! Elder Stanford, turn your eyes away.

Elder Stanford *looks away, then, holding a book over his face, he takes a little furtive peep out.*

Mick (*hopeful*) Well, I guess this is it, lads. I do appreciate you trying but . . .

He stops speaking as **Siobhan** *suddenly walks in the open door.*

Siobhan Hope you don't mind me being early, Mick, I . . . (*She stops dead, then points.*) My knickers!

Mick Good Jesus!

Elder Osborne Michael!

Siobhan *turns to leave and* **Mick** *grabs her. She pulls away but he manages to hold onto her.*

Mick I can explain, honest. (*To the* **Mormons**.) Lads, give me a break. (*They look at him.*) Come on, give me a minute to myself!

Reluctantly the two men retreat towards the door as **Mick** *leads* **Siobhan** *over beside the bed. She is deeply shocked, yet trying to stay cool.*

Siobhan I can't believe this, Mick. The only reason you took me in was probably to steal my underwear. Why bother with me? I mean I could have just sent them over in a plastic bag.

Mick (*embarrassed but pleading*) Come on, Siobhan, you know me better than that.

Siobhan I don't. I mean I've been sleeping with a transvestite. I can't take it, Mick, I just wish you'd told me.

Mick Give me a chance to explain, Siobhan. For the past three weeks I've had these fuckers up my arse. They're determined to convert me. I've tried everything else to get rid of them.

Siobhan Have you never just tried 'Go and fuck off'.

Mick Well, no, I mean I'm a man of sensibilities. I don't want to offend anybody. Now, you don't honestly think I'm a transvestite? Not somebody who follows Shelbourne?

Siobhan What about the old hatchet in here the other night?

Mick Stormtroopers from the Legion of Mary. The landlord called them in because of these boys. I'm desperate to be rid of the whole shagging lot of them.

Siobhan (*suddenly serious*) Swear to me you're telling the truth.

Mick (*looking down at his outfit*) Black and red – the Bohs colours? Do you have to ask?

Siobhan (*laughs*) You look ridiculous. Put some clothes on for God's sake and I'll sort these cowboys out.

He dresses while she goes over to the **Mormons** *beside the door.*

Siobhan (*firmly*) I'm afraid I'm going to have to ask you to leave. My friend is very upset just now and I think it would be better if you didn't call on him in future.

Elder Osborne I assure you our only thoughts are for his own welfare. Michael is in a dark night of the soul. Tell him we were not really shocked by his clothes. All these things are an attempt to escape from himself: the dressing up, the drugs, the drinking and the three little girls he had sleeping with him here one night last week.

Siobhan The three little what!

Elder Stanford (*helpfully*) Three sisters. Eh, schoolgirls I think.

He nods to **Elder Osborne**, *pleased to have been of assistance.*

Siobhan (*looking back*)　I'll show the bastard.

She returns to **Mick** *who is now almost fully dressed. He smiles at her, but she slaps him in the face, grabs her panties off the bed and storms out.*

Mick (*holding his face*)　What in God's name?

He looks at the two **Mormons**.

Elder Stanford (*reassuringly*)　Never mind Michael, you still have us.

Mick　Out!

They retreat as he approaches them menacingly, before **Elder Osborne** *rallies.*

Elder Osborne　Now now, Michael. This is a bad time for you but we'll stick in there. When you repent she'll come running back, anxious to join with you in the light of grace. There is a quotation here I would like to share with you.

He begins to search quickly through the pages of the large bible he carries while **Elder Stanford** *parks himself happily on the sofa. There is the sound of knocking on* **Bosco**'s *door.*

Mick (*weakly*)　Piteous Christ, lads, you're destroying my life.

Ollie (*from the hallway*)　Bosco! Are you a tad in, Bosco?

Elder Osborne　Ah, here we are, John, chapter . . .

There is a knock on the open door, silencing him. **Ollie** *and* **Pascal** *appear with two bags and a round wooden box.*

Ollie　Howya, you seen Bos . . .

Mick (*rushing forward in desperation to fling his arms around their shoulders*)　Cousin Oliver and little Pascal. Come to visit after all these years. Come in, come in.

He pulls **Pascal** *and* **Ollie** (*who look completely bewildered*) *into the room.*

Pascal   More bucking mushrooms?

Mick   You've come to stay, have you? It's marvellous
to see yous again. (*He turns to the* **Mormons**.) Sorry lads.
A family reunion. Fierce emotional. Eh, if you wouldn't
mind, it's a bit private.

Elder Stanford (*rising*)   Oh no, of course not.

Elder Osborne   John, chapter . . .

He looks in irritation at **Elder Stanford** *who is shaking
hands all round and heading for the door, then slams the book
shut, and reluctantly shakes hands with* **Ollie** *and* **Pascal**
before he too exits. **Mick** *closes the door behind the* **Mormons**
in relief and turns.

Mick   Sorry about that, lads. Drastic action called for.

Ollie   Not at all Mickey, sure we're a tad delighted to
be asked.

Mick   What?

Ollie   I suppose you want the bed, do you? I'm a tad
tired.

Mick   Wait, no . . .

Ollie   Fair play to you. Really appreciate it. You'd get
a tad sick of Bosco's floor inside.

*He deposits the round box on the bedside table, drops his bag on
the ground and with a leap planks himself full length on the bed.
He stretches his boots out and snuggles down.*

Ollie   You're a tad fond of your comfort, aren't you?

Mick   I am. I was.

He watches **Pascal** *take off his boots, grab a packet of biscuits
off the bedside table and climb into the other side of the bed,
finding the bra, looking at it and then flinging it onto the floor.*
Pascal *and* **Ollie** *settle down contentedly for the night.* **Mick**
stares at them, sighs and then removes a tattered old sleeping bag

from the wardrobe and lays it out on the floor. He removes his shoes, trousers and top, then climbs into it.

Mick   How's Drogheda?

Ollie   Don't ask. A town in shagging crisis, the lowest point of the low.

Mick   More factory closures?

Ollie   Shag them. Local government elections!

Mick (*in sympathy*)   Holy wank!

Ollie   You can stick closures. You can stick the dole. But you know what local government elections mean?

Pascal (*splurts out*)   Bucking oul canvassers!

Ollie   Shagging posters of the bastards!

Pascal (*in one breath*)   Bucking handwritten notes done by bucking machine saying how bucking sad they were to have bucking missed you slipped in your bucking letterbox by bucking bastards doing the bucking hundred yard sprint down the bucking road.

Mick *looks visibly unnerved by* **Pascal**'s *speech.*

Ollie   Mobile advice clinics pissing past playing Wolfe Tone records.

Pascal   Bucking loudspeakers mounted on bucking cars.

Ollie   No. What kills me most is people being a tad nice to you. The oul bastard of a grocer on the corner of my street. He hates me. I hate him. We're grand. Then every six months there's another election and he starts smiling at me, asking about my mother, any sign of a job, saying he'll put a word in for me.

Mick (*wearily*)   It doesn't sound a good place to be, lads.

Ollie   It's not, but we've a wee tad of a plan, Pascal, don't we.

Pascal (*in a voice filled with nervous apprehension*)   Oh
Jaysus, don't bucking mention that!

*The lights go down for a brief period, then grow again, very
faintly to suggest that dawn is approaching. A flashlight held by*
Pascal *is shone and we see the outline of* **Ollie** *shoving the
round box under the bed.*

Ollie (*whispering as he rises*)   Are you right so?

Pascal (*whispering back*)   Call it off, Ollie. I'm bucking
petrified.

Ollie   Don't chicken out now.

They approach the sleeping figure of **Mick** *lying in the sleeping
bag near the armchair.* **Pascal** *kneels to wake him.*

Pascal   Mickey. We're just bucking off.

Mick (*sleepily*)   You're bucking what?

Pascal   We're away.

Mick (*relieved*)   Oh, great stuff.

Ollie *kneels beside him as well.*

Ollie   We're just leaving a wee tad of a parcel, Mick.
We'll collect it when we're back down in a few days'
time.

Mick (*confused*)   What? You're leaving what?

Ollie   Don't bother opening it, just leave it under the
bed. But look after it and don't go showing it to
anybody. I wouldn't even mention this to Bosco.

Mick (*waking up fully*)   Wait a second. What parcel?
Where?

Pascal (*rising*)   You're a bucking mate, Mick, so you
are. Bosco always said you were.

Pascal *and* **Ollie** *creep towards the door, which they open and* *exit in a thin blade of light.*

Mick (*completely awake and petrified*) Lads? Hang on a
second, lads. Let's talk about this.

The door shuts. **Mick** *scrambles up and switches on the light,
blinking in the force of it. He is naked except for a pair of
underpants. He looks around, then kneels by the bed to produce the
box.*

(*Lifting it out with trepidation.*) Buck me! (*He stops.*) Jaysus,
I'm starting to talk like them. If this isn't stolen it will
self destruct in three minutes.

Mick *rises and carefully places the box on the bedside chest of
drawers, above the secret panel. He bends his ear down to listen.*

I don't mind dying, I'd just hate being the first Irish
Mormon martyr. There'd be little plastercast statues of
me above doors all over Dublin. (*He raises his head.*) No
ticking. (*He stands back, considering.*) It's too quiet for a
smuggled piglet. Right!

*Standing to one side, he slowly cuts through the tape holding the
box together, then carefully lifts the lid. A look of horror covers his
face as gradually a crooked human head is revealed. He backs
away, tossing the lid of the box away from him in terror and
blesses himself.*

(*Mesmerised, speaking with difficulty.*) The head of Oliver
Plunkett! The head! (*He looks at the closed door and shouts.*)
Ye shagging bastards, ye shagging sacrilegious bastards!
You stole the head of Saint Oliver Plunkett. (*Pause, then a
shout of great indignity.*) And you left the shagging thing
with me!

*He sits on the edge of the bed, his hands shaking, his eyes glued to
the head in disbelief.*

This can't be true. God, I need a cigarette. And a
drink.

He searches in the drawer for a half-finished naggin of whiskey, which he lifts to his lips and swallows hard, before placing the bottle down on the table beside the head. His hands still shaking, he reaches for his jacket, takes out his cigarettes and, with difficulty, lights one. He inhales deeply, blows the smoke out and stares at the head. Slowly the eyes swivel to look at him.

The Head (*in a Scottish accent, with a voice as deep as the grave*)   Well, don't offer them around. Can you no see I've a mouth on me too?

Mick *shudders, his whole body convulsed with terror. Slowly,* **Mick** *takes the cigarette from his mouth and, as if in a dream, reaches slowly over to place the cigarette in the mouth of the* **Head**. *The* **Head** *inhales deeply, then blows the smoke back towards* **Mick**'s *face.* **Mick** *removes the cigarette and reaching for the whiskey bottle, holds it out, offering it to the* **Head**.

The Head   Naaaaaah. I've no stomach for alcohol.

Mick *tilts the whiskey bottle back and swallows hard, as the lights go down.*

Act Two

Scene One

*The sound of music is heard from the flat beneath **Mick**'s, then* **Mick**'s *voice is heard through the darkness.*

Mick   Forty-six . . . forty-seven . . . forty-eight . . .

Light comes up on the bed-sit. The **Head** *rants like a crazied preacher in a strong Scottish accent while* **Mick** *has his head immersed in a basin of water on the floor.* **Mick**'s *appearance shows signs of his not having slept all night. Throughout the second act his appearance should continue to deteriorate from shock, drink, drugs and lack of sleep. The actor playing the* **Head** *(listed in the cast as a Scottish gentleman for surprise purposes) never leaves the hidden alcove built into the chest of drawers. When the trick box is placed on top of the secret panel, he slips his head into it before the lid of the box is removed. When the lid is placed back down, he withdraws his head into the chest of drawers and closes the panel before the box is lifted up again. The lighting suggests that it is early morning.*

The Head   Yea, weeping shall be heard from the mountain tops and eagles crisscross the sky . . .

Mick (*lifting his head with a splash of water*)   Forty-nine.

Mick *looks at the* **Head** *and when it begins to speak again, ducks his head back into the basin.*

The Head   . . . and blood run through the streets in torrents, vengeance washing over the shores, driving off the filth, the wicked and the damned . . .

Mick (*lifting head*)   Fifty. (*He stares at the* **Head** *which is just finishing talking.*) Good Jaysus! It's still doing it.

The Head   Blasphemer! In the presence of a saint . . .

Mick (*banging on the floorboards and shouting over the* **Head**'s *voice*)   Shut that fucking music up!

The Head   . . . Cursed be your seed and breed!

The music stops. **Mick** *sits back on his heels.*

Mick   Merciful hour.

The Head   A plague shall cover the land. Death stalking the streets as children run to embrace him. I say to you . . . (*He is convulsed by a fit of coughing and his tone switches to conversational.*) Will you no light up another one of those fags for God's sake?

Mick *rises to light a cigarette and place it in the* **Head**'s *mouth.*

Mick   I didn't know saints smoked.

The Head (*the cigarette drops from his mouth as he shouts*)   Didn't know! Quote me chapter and verse where it says saints shalt not smoke. I'll no argue the finer points of theology with you, ye pup ye!

Mick   I'm doing it again, talking back to it.

Mick *replaces the cigarette in the* **Head**'s *mouth, who puffs away contentedly as* **Mick** *rushes over to examine the piles of books on the floor, opening one and searching through it frantically.*

Mick   Hallucinogenic mushrooms. Time limits for flashback. (*He looks up.*) It must be them bloody farmers spraying chemicals.

The Head (*the cigarette falling from his mouth again as he resumes shouting in rhetorical tones*)   And plagues of locusts strip the grass from the soil. Lo, and I say unto you, there shall be tears shed . . .

There is the sudden loud droning of an alarm clock which further unnerves **Mick**. *He roots under the bed, takes it out, shakes it and kills the sound.*

Mick (*hitting his own head*)   Wake up! (*Stops.*) Shag it, I am awake. I'm in no fit state to work. It's the stress of visitors. Take to the bed. Cold turkey. No drink, no drugs. Do something drastic. Join a monastery, join the Swords branch of the Tidy Towns competition.

He places the clock on the floor and stares sternly at the **Head** *who is observing him.*

The Head (*crossly*) Will you no sit still when I'm talking to you?

Mick (*desperately*) Listen, I know you don't exist, but can you not stay quiet for five minutes even.

Mick *puts one finger to his lips, then opens the door cautiously.*

(*Calling politely.*) Bosco! (*No reply.*) Shay! (*Still no reply.*) Are any of yous bastards ever awake in the mornings? Anyone left in the world. (*He leans back against the wall.*) Alone in my agony.

The Head Are ye a man of faith or straw?

Mick (*to himself*) Don't answer it. It's a warning, like those blackouts last year.

The Head Take me to the multitudes and I will speak in tongues . . .

Mick Multitudes? (*He jumps forward.*) I have this licked.

He approaches the **Head** *who stops speaking and regards him critically.*

The Head No.

Mick No what?

The Head No to whatever is in your mind. I can smell the sin from here.

Mick I'm putting an end to this illusion right now.

The Head Enough talk! Prepare to go forth with my message.

Mick You're in my mind and nowhere else. Prove yourself.

The Head   Doubting Thomas! Would you put your fingers in the holes of the nails? What is this trial? I fear not your taunts!

Mick   Do you know what a telephone is?

The Head (*his voice drops to a whinge*)   Of course I know what a telephone is. We've had telephones for years in Drogheda. Why is everybody always slagging Drogheda?

Mick   Well then, just one phone call to say that I'm sick. Bad cold, won't be in till Wednesday. Do that and I'll believe in you.

The Head   Bad cold? There's nothing wrong with you that an honest day's work wouldn't cure. Besides I'm a saint. I can't be telling lies.

Mick (*catching himself on*)   What am I doing? Engaging it in conversation. (*He turns away.*) Put it back under the bed, go to work and then find those two bastards from Drogheda. Go to my doctor – wait, he just issues sick certs. Go to a real doctor.

He picks up the lid of the box and approaches the **Head**.

The Head (*worried*)   Bring me the phone.

Mick *stops with the lid suspended.*

Mick (*to himself*)   Don't do this to yourself, Mick. Not even for a day's sick.

Yet the tempation is too much. He weakly drops the lid onto the bed and goes to lift the **Head**.

The Head (*orders*)   Bring the phone to the door.

Mick   What?

The **Head** *glares at him, demanding to be obeyed.*

Mick   This is crazy. Walk out of here. (*Pulling himself together.*) No, kill this illusion now so you won't have to come back to it.

Mick *enters the hall where we hear him dial a number and then returns with the receiver on a long flex which he holds around the door. The* **Head** *opens his mouth to speak but the words come from a concealed tape recorder beside the door.*

The Head (*ultra posh, smarmy voice*) Hello. Mobile Libraries. I'd like to phone in sick for Michael Flaherty . . . yes, a severe head cold . . . thank you.

Mick *holds the receiver to his ear and listens.*

Mick Good Jaysus!

Mick *suddenly realises that the person at the other end hasn't rung off and clamps his hand over the mouthpiece. Gingerly he replaces the receiver in the hall and returns.*

The Head A marvellous machine.

Mick (*shocked*) He heard, he spoke to you. Jesus, you are real.

The Head I am not Jesus, but I am real and I have come with a mission in which you must play your chosen part.

Mick (*falling to his knees in terror*) What must I do, Master?

The Head Listen to my words. (*Voice changes.*) Nights in Drogheda cathedral with only the glow of the sanctuary lamp I have dwelt on these thoughts, letting this moment draw near. Now my silence has ended. My hand drew those thugs to desecrate the holy shrine and led them to this filthy spot, my hand chose you, the most wretched of creatures, to undertake my task. And now I charge you to deliver my message. Though men may scorn, enough will hear for its purpose.

Mick (*cowering*) Master, give me your words. Though the world declare me mad I'll stand on Dublin's bridges and preach to whoever will listen.

The Head No, you must travel to the cathedral steps

in my city of Drogheda and repeat my message there.

Mick Give me your words.

The Head Memorise them carefully. I have shaped them in my heart and now, through you, they shall be heard.

Mick (*intently, grabbing a pen and paper*) Go slowly please. I took woodwork instead of shorthand.

The Head I am the eye that has dwelt in the heart of your city, the nose that smelt your decay, the ears that have heard your teeming generations. Drogheda, I am your witness, observer of life and death. (*Louder.*) And I say unto you, ye have fallen from the heights of purity, drunk from the trough of greed, sinned against the rule of God, wallowed in filth like pigs in a sty. Promiscuity stalks the town, your women parade like the whores of Babylon. But it is time for repentance, time to cover the legs of your women folk. Time I came among you to guide and rule. (*He clears his throat as his voice changes from prophet to small-town politician.*) And so, after thirty decades of contemplation, I am putting myself forward for election to the city council and office of Lord Mayor. My people of Drogheda, on September the 13th, vote for me, Oliver Plunkett, saint and councillor, Independent Fianna Fail.

Mick (*throwing away the paper he has been writing on and springing to his feet to clamp the lid of the box quickly down over the* **Head**) Shag the Tidy Towns and the cold turkey – what I need is a joint!

He roots frantically under the bedclothes and produces a sliver of silver paper. He reaches under the bed and produces the Mormon book which now has no cover at all.

I don't believe it. No shagging roach paper!

There is a sudden pounding on the door.

Elder Osborne (*offstage*) Michael! Are your cousins

gone yet Michael?

Mick (*curling himself into a ball and staring at the dope in his hands*)   Shag the roach paper. I'll chew it raw!

Music starts again downstairs, as **Mick** *swallows the dope and the lights go down.*

Scene Two

The music fades out and lights come up to suggest midday. The lid has been removed from the box so that the **Head** *is exposed but the flat is otherwise empty. The door is open and we can see* **Mick** *in the hallway holding the telephone.*

Mick (*into the receiver*)   I got the number off Bosco. Of course I opened the shagging thing, have yous gone crazy? . . . Yes I know Drogheda is miserable, I know there's local elections . . . I don't want a cut, I just want yous to shift it from my room. I don't care what you do with it . . . Yes . . . And what did the bishop say when you phoned up? . . . He told you to what? Get away, where would a bishop learn a word like that? So what are you going to do . . . Yeah . . . yeah . . . and do what? WHAT? Now listen to me, Ollie, (*Shouts.*) you're a tad bucking crazy! Ollie? Ollie?

It's obvious that **Ollie** *has hung up.* **Mick** *replaces the receiver, enters the flat and bolts the door. He is carrying two books and a bottle of whiskey which he places on the bed. He sits, staring at the* **Head** *whose eyes suddenly swivel around to look at him.*

The Head   Well?

Mick (*jumps*)   Are you at it again?

The Head   Question not the mysteries of Mother Church. Better for ye to fall on your knees. A time will come when you will stalk the streets in rags, when the vermin and the lice shall shun you . . .

Mick Bucking Cassidy and the Tad-dance Kid want to cut your ear off.

The Head (*shocked*) Good Jaysus!

Mick The Drogheda Fox he's calling himself now. Mother Church don't place a high value on you. They were stunningly unconcerned. So the ear in the post is next.

The Head (*resigned*) Why not? What's another bit to me? Dig up my bones and shatter them. I'm sure you'll find a buyer for the dust. Another ear won't hurt.

Mick (*suddenly sympathetic*) I'm sorry.

The Head (*surprised*) What?

Mick I said I'm sorry. You were just landed on me.

The Head It's okay. Did you get fags?

Mick Oh. Here.

*He lights a cigarette, places it in the **Head**'s mouth and, having poured a large whiskey into a cup, begins to read one of the books beside him. The **Head** smokes contentedly for a moment.*

The Head You're great bloody company. Three centuries of silence and I get a bookworm. What is it anyway?

Mick A life of you.

The Head (*worried*) What are you reading that for?

Mick I'm approaching this scientifically. I know you're just a temporary apparition from stress that I'm going to exorcise with a mixture of alcohol and historical research.

The Head (*dismissively*) I wouldn't trust them books. Written years afterwards. Everything wrong in them.

Mick What was your mother's Christian name?

The Head   You never asked your mother personal questions in my day.

Mick   Then the name of your mother's cousin who became Bishop of Ardagh and Meath?

The Head (*in difficulty*)   Ah . . . Paddy?

Mick (*checking the book*)   A lucky guess. When did your sister Clare enter the convent in France?

The Head   When . . . when she attained the age of puberty, my son.

Mick (*reading*)   'Catherine, Anne, Mary.' (*He snaps the book shut in triumph.*) I'm rid of you. You never had a sister Clare. Or, at least, Oliver Plunkett never had. And furthermore, even allowing for periods abroad, there is no reference to him having had a Scottish accent. Now all I have to do is drink my way back to sanity and your voice will be gone.

The Head (*rants*)   Oh ye doubting Thomas, ye shall . . .

His voice trails off as **Mick** *waves the whiskey bottle in his face and he realises that he is having no effect.*

The Head (*quietly*)   Okay then, so I'm not Oliver Plunkett.

Mick (*surprised*)   Then who are you?

The Head (*wearily*)   George MacSpracken.

Mick   Who?

The Head   George MacSpracken. Formerly of Aberdeen. Twelve years a greengrocer in Greenwich.

Mick (*looking at the cup*)   I thought Jameson was a good whiskey.

The Head   I find it hard to believe myself. I thought I put six apples in the man's pouch. Well I didn't really, but there again I didn't know he was the king's tax collector. I mean the profit margin on apples was never large.

Mick (*to himself*)   Apples? Cider might work.

The Head   You'd probably get away with deportation now. But people were beheaded every afternoon for less in my day. Ah I saw Oliver from a distance in the tower. A fierce calm, brave man. Me, I was scared shitless and I was a simple beheading job – first offence, nothing fancy. It was sheer fluke it happened the same day. Never thought I looked like Oliver, but there again, have you ever seen anybody hung, drawn and quartered before? It took him hours to reach Tyburn, tied face-up on a sledge. I could hear the crowds as I waited my turn at the block, though God knows, I was only thinking of myself. Then I was thrust into position and only heard the executioner approach. (*Pause.*) It's strange, I thought there'd be a sharp wedge of pain and then nothingness, but the pain was so sudden it was just like a pinprick or a rush of air and then all dizzy lightness, the world turning upside down as my head rolled. But no more pain or fear ... like not being awake and yet aware of everything. (*Pause.*) A huge roar went up as Oliver's sledge arrived with the soldiers and the band. I was forgotten about, my head tossed under the wheels of a cart ... yet I was also up high, able to see everything ... the masked executioners, the crowd hushed as Oliver made his speech, their hunger for his slaughter. They hung him first till you'd think he was dead. But they knew their stuff and revived him for more pain, till the hangman finally hacked his head off and flung it into a bonfire. A priest managed to grab it and slip it under the cart where I was. There we were, eyeball to eyeball, me not knowing if he was dead, alive or in whatever class of limbo I was in myself, before, lo and behold, the priest hauls me out in his place. Give us a cigarette for God's sake. I hate remembering it.

Mick, *visibly unnerved, lights one in silence and places it to his* *lips. The* **Head** *inhales deeply.*

Mick (*to himself*)   This has got to be true. I'm too lazy to invent anything that complex.

The Head   I was just a thief. He was a good man.

Mick   Where's his head now?

The Head   Hopefully in whatever plot they buried the rest of me. He deserves a bit of peace and quiet. He'd endured enough shagging mutilation without having priests cart his limbs off to Germany and then Downside and his head to Drogheda. It's peace the dead need to be able to pass on. You try crossing over with people gawking in at you.

Mick   But life is a crock of shite and then you die. I mean that should be it.

The Head   It's no that simple or I could just vanish into oblivion.

Mick   Does it go on for ever?

The Head   Don't ask me. I've had no revelations or columns of angels, just the same thoughts circling round my brain.

Mick   But why did you never speak, tell somebody?

The Head   It only seems like days at times and then it feels like eternity. Do you believe in God? You'd think I'd know by now. Sometimes I think it's purgatory, my punishment that could last for ever. Other times I think I'm just a freak of nature. Often I sleep for decades or remember nothing and then the staring eyes are back. Always the same. Only the clothes change. The only way I know time has passed. Sometimes I lose the gift of speech, I'm too terrified to utter words or if I try people just shuffle away from the glass case.

Mick   But, surely there were priests. . . ?

The Head The clergy can be men of surprisingly little faith.

Mick What do you want?

The Head Oblivion. Peace. This old flat of yours is grand. Quiet.

Mick Ah now, don't be getting too comfortable. The nationwide hunt will start soon. I'm surprised they've managed to keep it quiet. They must have closed the cathedral.

The Head Not at all. Sure they've three papier mâché replicas of me. Often they stick one in when they bring me away for a hoover. How much are they asking for?

Mick Ten thousand in used notes.

The Head (*mocking laugh*) Big-time crooks. Even so they haven't a snowball's chance. The church does not pay out.

Mick Don't be knocking the church. They'll cough up yet. They've only another eighty thousand relics tucked away in vaults.

The Head Say what you like, but speaking as a communist, I've no time for them myself.

Mick (*astonished*) A what?

The Head A communist. Marxist-Leninist.

Mick Communism wasn't even invented when you were robbing the Greenwich proletariat.

The Head I haven't waited three centuries just to talk to some lazy sod like you. Back in the 1930s we had an excellent sacristan, a self-taught man. He used to read at night, hide the books away if any priest came in. Oh, in the end I just couldn't stand the curiosity. 'Give us a look' I shouted one night. Almost killed the poor fellow, but fair play. He was an atheist himself, but well read in the sciences. He took it in his stride when he got used to me. Even had a theory about my state being caused by the movement of capital. But I tell you, I got the bigger shock when he began reading to me. *Das Kapital* from cover to cover, *The Ragged-Trousered Philanthropist* – a darling of a book, *The Communist Manifesto*, my God, the ideas! We spent years at it, reading and discussing. Introduced me to the Woodbine too – a far better class of cigarette than those yokes. Only thing we couldn't agree on was Trotsky. I thought he was a decent bloke, but the sacristan was fierce inflexible about the party line.

Mick   What was he doing as a sacristan?

The Head   Infiltrating. Wormed his way into everything, the Legion of Mary, Vincent de Paul, tried to join the Blueshirts and the IRA. When Comrade Stalin comes he'll need the names, he'd say. He'd the biggest funeral for a layman I ever saw, and afterwards the only person who ever had an idea about me was his young son, and even then I could be wrong. But whenever the boy scouts filed past, singing 'Faith of our Fathers' I was always convinced that just when his son got to me he'd hum the 'Internationale'.

Mick   So what was all this preaching and damnation?

The Head   Sure I was more terrified than you. It's bad enough coming back to life without being an imposter. Besides, whatever chance I had of getting through to you with fire and brimstone I'd have shag all with 'Workers of the World Unite'.

Mick   The voice on the telephone?

The Head   A ventriloquist. Did a novena to me at the turn of the century.

Mick   Okay then, Independent Fianna Fail?

The Head   Infiltrate. Comrade Stalin will need the names.

Mick   Comrade Stalin is dead.

The Head   Shag that so. Anyway I thought I pitched it a bit liberal for Independent Fianna Fail.

There is a sudden knock.

(*Scared.*) They've come for me already. They heard.

Mick *places the lid back over the box.*

Mick (*politely*)   Who is it?

Siobhan (*offstage*)   Mick, I only have a few minutes for my lunch. I need to talk to you.

Mick *looks in confusion at the box, unable to make up his mind. She knocks again. He lifts it and puts it under the sofa (but where the audience can see it), then opens the door.* **Siobhan** *enters, trying to stay calm, but still shaken by what happened the previous night.*

Siobhan (*grins*)   Hi. Michelle, is it?

Mick   Give me a break, Siobhan.

Siobhan   I'm only teasing. (*Pause.*) What kept you so long though . . . opening the door? Were you. . . ?

She pauses uncertainly.

Mick   Was I what?

Siobhan (*tentatively*)   Dressing?

Mick (*baffled*)   Dressing? (*Her meaning registers.*) Ah listen, Siobhan, you got last night all wrong.

Siobhan   Mick, it's okay. You don't have to be bashful. I've been asking around, finding out about this. I mean it was a shock, but it's a big world. (*Pause.*)

Mick, I want to help you.

Mick   Oh Jaysus, not you as well! What happened to (*Sings.*) 'Girls just want to have fun'?

Siobhan   Come on, Mick, it's not easy on me coming here. I just want to clear up one question. Those girls?

Mick   What girls?

Siobhan   The three sisters or whatever you call them. Were they . . . you know?

Mick (*baffled*)   What do I know?

Siobhan   Well, were they girl girls or boy girls?

Mick (*putting his hands to his head as he collapses onto the sofa*)   I don't believe this. I am hallucinating.

Siobhan (*sitting beside him*)   I hear you just put on dresses and sit round calling each other Shirley and Monica. If you were simply just all being girls together I could forgive you, Mick. Naturally it wouldn't be like before, but we could still be good friends. Now what do you say?

Her foot kicks against the box and she glances down beneath the sofa before looking up with a knowing smile.

Siobhan   So what's in the box?

Mick (*springing up*)   Nothing! Leave it alone.

She falls to her knees with curious excitement.

Siobhan   It's your dresses, isn't it. Show them to me, Mick. Come on, let's bring this out into the open.

She lifts up the box and goes to open it. **Mick** *tries to grab it from her hands.*

Siobhan   Let me go, Mick, you're hurting! Please, let's be honest with each other!

Mick (*wrestling the box free*)   Just leave it, Siobhan! It's not dresses, it's . . .

There's a pause, while she looks at him.

Siobhan What?

Mick (*weakly*) It's private.

Siobhan I'm trying here, Mick. Listen, give me time.
Maybe it might even be all right between us, it could
even be fun. But you've got to be open with me, not
hiding away in your little world. What's the point of my
coming if you won't be honest. (*Pause.*) Mick, please
open the box. You've got to come out some time.
(*Pause.*) Open it now, Mick, or I'm going.

Mick *stands, clutching the box, trying to think of something to
say.*

Siobhan All right then, I'm sorry for you but it's
goodbye, Mick.

Siobhan *walks to the door, pausing for a last look back at him
before exiting. She closes the door on his silent misery.*

Mick Shag it! (*He puts the box back down on the secret
opening and removes the lid.*) I suppose you heard all that?

The Head Once life begins kicking you in the face it
just keeps on doing it.

Mick Well, come on then.

The Head Come on what?

Mick Proffer me advice. Everybody else does.

The Head (*dismissively*) I will in my bollocks You can
dance through the streets in a kimono for all I care.

Mick Convert me then. Let's get it over with.

The Head (*puzzled*) Convert you to what?

Mick Communism, Catholicism, whatever you're
having yourself.

The Head (*snorts*)   Give over that shite.

Mick   Aren't you worried for my welfare? Don't you wish me well?

The Head (*evil glint*)   I wish you'd roll another joint.

Mick (*grins suddenly*)   You know, I could get to like you.

Mick *lights a cigarette, places it in the* **Head***'s mouth and reaches for his coat. He puts it on.*

Mick   I'm getting some fresh air. See if that might banish you.

The Head   Out?

Mick   Social intercourse with human beings with actual bodies. Remember?

The Head (*plaintively*)   Don't leave me.

Mick   What?

The Head   Don't leave me again so soon. I've been such a long time alone in that cathedral. Stay. Please.

Mick   Listen, I'm . . .

The Head   Please.

Mick *stares at him, then begins to take his coat off again.*

Mick   I don't believe this. My life is destroyed and you're making me feel guilty. I never felt guilty about anything. The only people I ever felt sorry for were those Mormons and look where it got me. Guilt. I hate that. And you're doing it.

The Head (*cajoling*)   I knew you'd be a good lad, kind to an old person.

Mick   Shut up. (*Looks around.*) What'll we do for the afternoon?

The Head (*with a sly grin*)   Poker.

Mick   You play poker?

The Head   Not very well. Just straight. (*Pause after each name.*) And Five-Card Stud. And Seven-Card. And Southern Cross. And Klondiky. And Blind Baseball.

Mick   Get away.

The Head   A reformed gambler in the 1940s had a great devotion to me. Loan an old man five pounds, will you? My mind is befuddled but sure you can keep winning it back.

Mick   Okay. Okay. Straight poker, jacks to open.

Mick *reaches in his pockets to produce a crumpled fiver which he places down beside the* **Head***. He pours himself another whiskey and takes up a deck of cards from the bedside locker.*

The Head   You deal. And roll us a blast of the good stuff.

Mick *looks round, then props a toast rack sideways in front of the* **Head** *and places five cards on it, facing the* **Head***.*

The Head   I'll open for a pound. Two cards please. The last two. (**Mick** *goes to remove them.*) No looking to see what they are.

Mick (*giving him new cards*)   I don't cheat. The sooner those spacers return you the better.

The Head   Sure the whole thing happened before. I'll raise you fifty quid.

Mick   You only have a fiver. When?

The Head   A mad Black-and-Tan made off with me back in 1921. The bet is fifty pounds, you'll see my money when you see my hand.

Mick   I thought all Black-and-Tans were mad. (*He shows his cards.*) Two pair.

The Head   This fellow was by the time I'd finished

with him. A house of jacks.

Mick   On your first hand? Very dodgy George. Had he any joy?

The Head   Not a tosser . . . he left me back at dead of night. Where's me fifty quid?

Mick (*dealing again*)   I don't have it. (*Looks around.*) Take the television.

The Head   You better not only get RTÉ. (*Pause.*) Mick?

Mick   What?

The Head   Don't send me back.

Mick   What am I supposed to do with you?

The Head   Anything. Just don't send me back to those gaping eyes. Bury me in a hole, put me in the fire. It would just be a moment's pain and then maybe oblivion. Okay, I might still exist as a speck of ash, but I'll take that risk. Just don't send me back.

Mick   Listen, I had a grand life before you, the Mormons, the Legion of Mary and half of Drogheda descended on me. As soon as possible I'm getting you off my hands and from there on it's your problem, George. Now can you open?

The Head   Please, Mick.

Mick   I'm piling the furniture in front of that door, taking to the bed with a packet of Alpen, a twenty spot of dope, a softback edition of *Lord of the Rings* and the world can go and shite. No offence, comrade. Now yes or no? How many cards?

The Head   I'll open, one card. Think about it, Mick. All those years of faces clouding the glass, hoping for cures.

Mick (*uncomfortable*)   Just play the cards, George. Stop putting your life on my shoulders.

The Head   Petrified children backing away ... Raise you fifteen quid.

Mick   The blankets are worth twenty. I'll see you for five.

The Head   What am I suppose to do with blankets?

Mick   What are you going to do with a television when you're back in your glass case? (*Shows his cards.*) Three nines.

The Head   Don't mention that kip. A house, fives and sevens.

Mick   Ye bollocks. How do you do it?

The Head   How could I cheat? I don't even have hands.

Mick   You're still going back. Do you hear?

His voice drops to a whisper as footsteps approach the door. There is a knock and **Shay***'s voice is heard.*

Shay (*offstage*)   No post at all this evening, Mick. What more proof do you want? Don't forget the poker session tonight.

Mick *and the* **Head** *stare furtively at each other, until the footsteps retreat.*

Mick   Here, shag this, take the whole flat. I need a kip before these boys arrive and (*He sniffs under his armpit.*) a shower.

The Head   We never needed showers in my day ...

Mick (*lifting up the lid of the box*)   I hate to break it to you, George, but you do now!

In the flat below 'The Cards of the Gambler' begins to play as **Mick** *lowers the lid and the stage plunges into darkness.*

Scene Three

There is the noise of running water, then of knocking, growing louder. **Mick** *emerges from the shower in silhouette in rapid jerky movements like a speeded-up film. He answers the door and* **Bosco** *and* **Shay** *enter at the same speed, carrying six-packs as they settle down to open the bottles and play cards. The record dies as the lights come back up, with the fire obviously lit in the fireplace.* **Mick** *is just wearing jeans, has a towel around his neck and his hair looks wet. They are playing cards on the coffee table.* **Shay** *sits on the sofa,* **Bosco** *on a small stool and* **Mick** *in the bed. The box has been moved to where we can see it under the bed. They are arguing. The six-packs around them are in active use.*

Shay We almost had to break the door down. You must have been having a good time in here with *The Sacred Heart Messenger*.

Mick Don't be slagging *The Sacred Heart Messenger*. My mother attracted the da through it.

Bosco What? Did she advertise?

Mick No, she wet the cover and rubbed the red ink on her face as rouge. I told you, Shay, you caught me in the shower.

Shay I thought you'd finally cracked up. Too many black-and-white movies in the afternoon. Every time the sun shines you close the curtains, put on the electric fire and stick your head in a book or watch *Bilko* or *Bonanza*. You'll go blind.

Mick My afternoons are always quiet. Can anybody open?

All mutter 'No' and throw their cards back in.

Mick Stoke the pot. Kings or better.

Bosco You'd be better off buying a video, watch something good like *ET*.

Shay (*snorts*)   That Cavan bastard. Ah come on, Mick. Just once play something else.

Mick   House rules. Poker variations only. Dealer's choice.

Bosco   How could ET be a Cavanman?

Shay   Sure, doesn't he look like one. Right, deal them so.

Mick   Don't mention Cavanmen. Did I ever tell you about the time I stopped for a pint in Bailieborough?

Shay   You did not. Now just deal, will you, I'd like to actually finish a hand.

Mick (*dealing*)   I ordered a pint of Guinness in a pub there and I'm drinking away, minding me own business when this local walks in and says to the barman, (*Cavan accent.*) 'Giz a pint of rat, Joe.'

Shay   Me granny!

Mick   So the barman takes this dead rat from the fridge, stuffs it in a pint glass, fills it with water and hands it to him. Your man throws it back straight, slaps the glass down, and orders 'Another pint of rat, Joe.'

Bosco   Beats shagging Murphy's anyway.

Mick   So he says to me, 'What's the Guinness like?' 'Grand,' I said, 'How's the rat?' 'Best pint of rat in the county,' he says. 'Men come from miles to have it.' So I thought, shag this, I'll try it and I say to the barman, 'Throw us on a pint of rat.' Well he takes this big one out, but I'm starting to get cautious now, so I say 'I'll just have a glass to start.' Anyway the barman can't fit the rat into the small glass so he bites its head off, shoves the rest of the body in and fills it up with water. 'Well you can shag off,' I said to him, 'I'm not drinking that . . .'

Bosco   Quite right too.

Mick   '. . . There's no bleeding head on it!'

Shay *laughs and looks down at his hand.*

Shay   Can anybody open? Change the game, Mick. Klondiky, Seven-Card Stud, Southern Cross, they're all poker variations. Why do you always deal straight?

Mick   I like it.

Shay   But nobody can ever shagging open.

Mick   That's why I like it. Aces high. Stoke the pot. (*They throw more money in.*) What the hell is that, Bosco?

Bosco   Butter vouchers. They're worth 55p each.

Shay (*indignant*)   There's no rule in poker says we have to accept butter vouchers.

Bosco   What's wrong with them? Do you not eat butter? Do you not have toast in the morning?

Mick *shuffles and deals again.*

Shay   Of course I've shagging toast. I eat Weetabix, then I have shagging toast, but I'm still not accepting butter vouchers in the pot. Now are we playing cards or talking?

Bosco   You're lucky to be able to afford Weetabix. Try that on the dole. One pound ninety-seven, down in the twenty-four hour shop.

Mick (*interrupting*)   I've had a trying day, lads. I'd like a bit of relaxation. Can anybody open?

Shay   That's bleeding robbery. They're only one pound thirty-five in The Shopping Basket.

Mick   Ace high lads. Openers?

Bosco   Well Super Crazy Prices is the best place. I know you have to walk across town to get there, but one pound nineteen. I mean is that value or is that value?

Shay Robbing bastards in the twenty-four hour. What do you think of the new Alpen?

Mick (*shouts*) Can yous open?

They look down.

Shay *and* **Bosco** No.

Mick Stoke the pot, no butter vouchers. Kings high. What are you putting in now, Bosco?

Bosco *has thrown a packet onto the table.*

Shay Ohhhh – johnnies. The hard man, Bosco.

Mick You roll them down over your dick, Bosco. You don't use them in poker.

Bosco I'm broke. They're worth a pound anyway.

Mick What are you doing with johnnies anyway? Is the teddy bear afraid of getting Aids.

Bosco No, for the dope.

Shay What?

Bosco So I could stick the dope inside one and swallow it if the cops arrived.

Mick Good Jaysus. All right, going cheap for a pound. Will somebody roll a number?

Shay You don't swallow Blu-Tack, Bosco, you just stick it under your tongue.

All laugh except **Bosco**.

Bosco Bitch never showed up! Took my money and all.

Shay All you had to do was knock. I've the best of stuff. (*He looks down.*) Shite, there's a fly in my drink.

Shay *roots around the lip of his bottle with his finger as everyone throws money into the pot.* **Mick** *deals again as* **Shay** *holds his* *finger up, examining the fly on it. He squeezes his finger.*

Shay (*to the fly*)   Spit it back out, you thieving bastard! (*Flicks the fly away and reaches into his jacket to take out a piece of hash in silver foil.*) Five-Card Stud then. Blind Baseball. Why do you keep doing this to us, Mick?

Bosco   It's awful that, getting a pint with no head.

Mick   Just open, Bosco, right.

Bosco (*glancing at his cards*)   I can't. Anyway those lads who were here in the dark suits thought that I got a good deal for the size of it.

Shay   You mean the headbangers from Drogheda who've been camped on your floor for the past month?

Bosco   No. The two fellows who are in here with Mick every second afternoon. They look like they've a few bob on them. You should ask them to hang on for a poker session some night, Mick.

Shay   I don't know them.

Mick (*embarrassed*)   They're nobody. Shut bleeding up, Bosco.

Bosco   You must know the lads in the suits and dark glasses. Nice guys. They were asking me where I got the thirty-spot and I think they said they were planning to give you a call.

Shay (*his paranoia returning*)   What suits and glasses?

Mick   I'll murder you, Bosco.

Shay   You shut up, Mick. Keep talking, Bosco. Who are these boys?

Bosco   Ah, they're just mates of Mick who often call in to him for a chat. Posh-looking lads with short hair in dark suits.

Shay   It's the Branch. (*Stands up.*) The bleeding Special

Branch. You're a grass aren't you? My God, I'm playing cards with you and you're passing on every scrap of information. And I used to supply you cheap too!

Mick   Shay, will you sit down. It's not the police. They're just friends, they're Mor . . .

Shay   You're dead, do you hear me! Don't try and tell me anybody who owned a suit would be a friend of yours, let alone (*Pointing to* **Bosco**.) talk to that spare.

Bosco   I had a suit once!

Shay   And the judge called you the accused. (*To* **Mick**.) I'm getting my gear and those plants out of here, but I've got friends, right, and the boys in the trenchcoats will come looking for you one of these nights. (*He darts forward to grab* **Mick***'s kneecap.*) Black-and-Decker, Black-and-Decker.

He exits leaving **Mick** *speechlessly looking at* **Bosco**. *There is a moment's silence before* **Bosco** *suddenly begins to laugh.*

Bosco   There's no bleeding head on it! I get it now. That's your best one yet. (*Puzzled.*) Jaysus, Shay got fierce narkey.

Mick (*rising*)   Get out! Just leave me alone.

Bosco *backs away towards the door with* **Mick** *advancing on him. But just as he reaches it there's a knock and* **Bosco** *opens it.*

Bosco   Ah howya, lads. We were just talking about you.

Bosco *exits and the* **Mormons** *enter.*

Elder Osborne   That's the stuff, Michael. Spreading the word among your friends!

Mick   Just piss off, right, leave me alone.

Elder Osborne (*tuts*)   Language, Michael, and cards and drink. Still trying to fight yourself. Don't give up

now when we were making such good progress. (*Firmly.*)
To business. I think we had dealt with most of your
historical problems about polygamy the evening when
you had to go off to your embalming classes but I
detected a few reservations about the twelve apostles
which Christ chose from among the Nephites after he
came from Palestine to America. (*They both take their seats
on the sofa.*) Well, to continue our discussion I would like
to read to you from . . .

Shay *appears around the door with a carrier bag in one hand
and a puny hash plant in the other.*

Shay (*shouts*)   Dead, do you hear me, dead.

He sees the **Mormons** *and stops.*

Elder Stanford (*rising eagerly to greet him*)   But born
again in the immersion of Baptism.

Shay   Good Jaysus, even the police have found God.

He exits quickly.

Elder Osborne (*scowling at* **Elder Stanford** *as he
reaches into his briefcase for a book*)   The Nephites. When
Christ reached America after his resurrection once again
he had to choose . . .

Mick   No, I said out! You're like vultures around my
neck. Before I met yous I had friends, I had a woman,
I . . .

Elder Stanford   Had you found your way to God?

Mick   No! And I'll find it by my shagging self. You're
all the same, Mormons, Jehovahs, Catholics, Moonies,
circling round, looking for weaknesses. That's what you
want, people too terrified to make decisions, people so
stunned that anybody gives a fuck about them that
they'd jump into the Liffey if you asked.

Elder Osborne   Elder Stanford and I . . .

Mick You're not elders, you're bleeding nippers. I'm five years elder than the pair of yous. Listen, I've seen your converts, middle-aged men in suits having orgies of ice cream, following the rules for an Apex ticket to heaven. Don't tell me about sin. I'll tell you, I've lied and cheated, I'd ride a nun's arse through a church railing, but whatever the fuck is out there when I keel off this planet I'll face It or Him or Her or Nothingness in my own way on my own way on my own.

Mr Lewis (*offstage*) There's two weeks' rent due. Shamus! And what about that ESB bill? Come back here, you owe me money.

Shay (*offstage*) Let me go! This place is crawling with shagging cops!

Mr Lewis (*offstage*) And I'm one of them.

Shay *storms into the room, pursued by* **Mr Lewis**. **Shay** *ignores everyone, walks straight across the bed and stands by the window furtively trying to eat the leaves of his dope plant.* **Mr Lewis** *stands confronting the* **Mormons**.

Elder Stanford Good evening sir.

Mr Lewis I've warned you before, Mickey. Have you no sense, boy?

Mick Do you mind if I fix you up next week?

Bosco *appears eagerly at the door.*

Bosco What's this? Another poker session already?

He is pushed into the room by **Lily** *and* **Jack** *who appear suddenly in the door.*

Lily (*advancing*) There they are, sneaking in! I had Jack at the end of the road watching out for yous.

Jack (*closing the door behind him*) Aye. It beats sitting in these evenings.

Lily Well, you can take your hands off him, because

he's a one-hundred per cent good Catholic boy and he'll never be anything else. (*She grabs hold of* **Mick**'s *arm.*) Do you hear?

Elder Osborne   Michael is an intelligent boy. Let him make his own mind up. We'll have no kidnapping here. (*He grabs* **Mick**'s *other arm.*) Don't worry, Michael, we're here to protect you.

Mr Lewis   And I'll have the last four weeks' rent if you don't mind.

As he makes a dive for **Mick**'s *pocket there is a loud knock on the door which freezes everyone.*

Mick (*puzzled*)   I don't know anybody else.

Lily *and* **Elder Osborne** *release* **Mick** *and he opens the door to a* **Stranger** *in a long trenchcoat standing in the hallway. The angle of the door means that he cannot see the crowd inside.*

Stranger (*Northern Ireland accent*)   Are you Michael? (**Mick** *nods. The* **Stranger** *continues darkly.*) A 'friend' asked me to pay you a call.

Mick (*backing away scared and calling*)   Shay, I like my kneecaps as they are.

Stranger   I work with Siobhan in the tax office.

Mick (*with intense relief*)   You're from the . . . tax office . . .

Stranger   Why shouldn't I be? We're not *all* scruffy-haired beatniks in the tax office, you know.

Mick   Listen, this is just a bad time.

Stranger   I know all about it, you poor lad. Siobhan came to me for advice, you see, the girls often do. I mean they're only human, it's hard for them to understand some things. She asked me to apologise to you. It was the shock she said, but, and these are her words, you are what you are and she knows you are a good person at heart. She gave me these for you. Herself and all her friends spent the afternoon choosing them in Penney's. (*He hands* **Mick** *a parcel.*) I suggested the undies with the pink lace, I hope you like those especially.

Mick Ah hang on now, just who the hell are you?

Stranger Sean, but my friends call me Sharon, the topless waitress! (*He drops his overcoat to reveal a French maid's outfit which leaves most of his chest exposed.*) And you can too! Sure we're all girls together!

Mick Holy wank!

Mick *steps back in shock and the* **Stranger** *enters, seeing the group gathered on the far side of the room.*

Stranger (*shocked*) Auntie Lily!

Lily (*hysterical*) My little Sean! A Jehovah's Witness!

Jack (*consoling*) A topless waitress love, a topless waitress.

Lily Oh thanks be to God!

Stranger I can't hide it any longer, Aunt Lily. I'm a TV.

Mick At least you're not a PD.

Jack Hello, Sean.

Stranger Hello, Uncle Jack.

Jack Will this hobby last longer than the wine-making?

Stranger Don't be cruel now, Uncle Jack.

Lily A waitress. I need a cup of tea. None of my family were ever in service before. (*She sits down.*) Tell me, Sean, you haven't lost the faith?

Stranger Of course not, Aunt Lily. Sure where else

would you get the fashions. Here, I'll be mother.

The **Stranger** *begins to fill the kettle.*

Elder Stanford Just hot water for me please.

Elder Osborne (*sitting down to take* **Lily***'s hand*) You poor woman. The shame of it.

Lily You see them come into the world, you raise them up . . .

Elder Osborne Oh I know . . . the pain of it too.

Jack (*going over to the* **Stranger**) How's the mother keeping, Sean?

Stranger The very best, Uncle Jack.

Elder Stanford *seems transfixed by the* **Stranger** *and follows his every move, gazing intently at him.*

Lily (*to* **Elder Osborne**) He was always such a good boy. (*She looks over at the* **Stranger**.) Could you not cover yourself up, Sean, get a nice modest dress. There are some lovely ones in Clery's.

Stranger (*coming over to her*) I know the very ones you mean, Aunt Lily.

Lily Good material. To keep you warm in winter.

Elder Osborne It's very important that in your climate.

Lily Oh I imagine it can be very cold standing on doorsteps.

Elder Osborne Well, of course, we only use the very best material.

He lets **Jack** *and the* **Stranger** *feel the lining on his jacket.*

Jack Powerful material. I remember during the emergency when you couldn't get cloth for love or money . . .

Mick *has been watch all this happen without anyone paying him the slightest attention. Now he shouts suddenly.*

Mick   Right! Every one of yous, out of my flat now!

There is a stunned silence.

Lily   Just a moment, young man. I didn't come here to be insulted.

Mick   I don't give a shite why you came here . . .

Elder Osborne   Michael! That's no way . . .

Jack (*interrupting*)   Listen here, son, you can't just walk in here and start using language to my wife.

Mick   I live here. This is my home. It's you that's after walking in.

Lily   But only for your own good.

Elder Osborne   We had you down as a chronic case, Michael, but I never knew you needed our help this bad.

Mick   God, save me from those who want to do me good. You even have that sawn-off gauleiter at it now. (*He points to* **Mr Lewis**.) We had a fine relationship before, (**Mr Lewis** *smiles in agreement*.) he simply exploited me.

Mr Lewis (*frowns*)   What do you mean?

Mick   Now even he wants to do me good. If you want to do me good then leave me alone. Can't you see that all I want is to be left to myself . . . to eat scuttery kebabs, white bread and scabby packets of soup with E's in them, to read books in Latin and watch Open University programmes at five in the morning about frogs fucking and the homosexual tendencies of the ten-spined stickleback. To do . . . I don't know . . . anything except be a part of whatever the hell you're all into. (*Pause.*) Listen, I'm going to die, I've x number of years left. I'd like to get on with them in my own way and own time, so it's very nice of yous, but it's none of your business. Now good night and thanks for calling.

There is a silence as everybody stares at him.

Mr Lewis (*drawing himself up to his full height*) I'll not stay here to be insulted. You owe me three weeks' rent, Bosco Ignatius.

Bosco *heads for the door with* **Mr Lewis** *in pursuit and* **Shay** *making a break for it behind them.*

Jack God, you've a fine voice, son. You wouldn't think of coming down to the local Fianna Fail cumann.

Stranger (*to* **Lily**) It's dear for dresses Clery's though.

Lily (*to* **Elder Osborne**) You despair of helping some people. Well, I'll not have Irish hospitality abused. The Legion House is only around the corner if anybody would like a good strong cup of tea.

Stranger I'd love a cup, Aunt Lily.

Elder Stanford *is still staring at the* **Stranger**. *Now he plucks up courage, touches the* **Stranger**'s *bare arm and speaks in a voice which has dropped its textbook authority and is filled with childish wonder.*

Elder Stanford What does it taste like . . . as it slides down your throat?

The room is transfixed by the question.

Stranger What?

Elder Osborne Tea.

Mick (*roars*) Out!! Everyone! Go and save somebody else.

They all rise and troop, bristling with wounded expressions, past **Mick** *who stands by the door.* **Jack** *is the last to leave. He pauses beside* **Mick**, *about to start a friendly chat.*

Jack It's been great getting out in the evenings. Sure, I could call round myself some time for an oul chat . . .

Mick *shoves him out the door and slams it. He draws the two bolts shut and leans against the door frame. There is silence for a moment, before a loud knock startles him. He jumps, holding the back of his head as if it had received a blow.*

Ollie Hey, you in there, we're a tad in a hurry. We've come for the yoke.

Mick What?

Ollie Open up, Mick. All we need is the ear. We'll leave you the rest if you want.

Mick *stares at the box under the bed, clearly trying to make his mind up about something. He looks back at the door, rubbing his hands nervously. Then he rushes over to grab the box and hurls it into the heart of the fire. A large spurt of flame shoots up, its reflection lighting the stage, while* **Pascal** *and* **Ollie** *pound on the door.* **Mick** *stares at the fire, then rises and draws the bolts back. He opens the door.*

Ollie (*entering*) Jaysus, what kept you?

Mick I had something to do.

Ollie They stuck another head in its place. Would you believe it? But the severed ear is bound to work. They'll not outsmart the Drogheda Fox. We'll give you a wee tad of a cut, Mick. We were always going to. Where is it?

Mick *points to the fire.* **Ollie** *and* **Pascal** *rush towards it.*

Pascal There's the bucking box. Buck it. (*He tries to reach it with his hands, but is unable to.*) A poker? Have you a bucking poker?

Ollie (*grabbing* **Mick**) You, you spacer, you animal. Have you a poker?

Mick No.

Ollie (*throwing* **Mick** *violently onto the bed*) Murderer. You bad bastard. We were always going to put it back, no matter what. They could have glued the ear back on. Have you not got a tad of respect for anything? Have you no respect for culture, for the past, no respect for your heritage? If it's one thing I hate it's you city slickers with your pluralist society, kinky sex and rock and roll. Well, I'm proud to be an Okie from Muskogee. That's my culture you're burning.

Pascal (*kneeling beside the fireplace*) The head of Oliver Plunkett burning. (*He crosses himself.*) Saint Oliver, we didn't mean any bucking harm. We were only . . . and it was all Ollie's idea . . . (*He thinks.*) Drogheda. Bucking Drogheda without the bucking head. You take away the head and what have you left? Buck all. Oh, nobody will know, but I will. When I walk down the town and look into the cathedral I'll know it's gone, gone for ever. (*He turns to* **Ollie** *who is attempting to strangle* **Mick** *on the bed.*) I can't bucking watch the box burst open. Jesus, it's disintegrating. Oh the bucking box is bucking bucked . . . buck it!

Pascal *runs from the room.* **Ollie** *sees him go, takes one terrified look at the fireplace and then races after him.* **Mick** *picks himself off the bed with difficulty and goes over to close the door. He draws the bolts again and limps towards the fireplace, hunching down to stare reflectively into the flames. There is silence.*

The Head (*speaking from the shower*) Fair play to you, son. I knew you wouldn't let me down. (*Pause.*) But if you don't dry me off soon I'll get me death of cold in this shower.

Mick *rises and goes to the shower unit. He comes out with his back to the audience, carrying something, and places it down on the table. When he steps back the* **Head** *is there, very wet-looking and blindfolded.*

The Head Your modesty is touching, Mick, but I have seen a dick before.

Mick I'm particular about who I share my shower with.

He takes the blindfold off and starts to dry the **Head**.

Mick You're on probation, do you hear me? You shower more than once every three centuries for a start.

The Head I survived long enough without . . .

Mick And cheat again at cards and you're going back to that cathedral in a basket.

The Head Stop accusing me of cheating, Mick. I have feelings too. Besides if you don't, I won't show you how it's done.

Mick Do you think I'll ever be sane again? I mean I must be crazy, but I'm starting to prefer your company, George.

The Head We're two of a kind, Mick. The little men of history, unimportant, overlooked, just getting on with living as best we can. You've only been hounded for three weeks. I've been hounded for three centuries. But it's a great rest we'll have now, and great sleeping in the long nights after Samhain. Just the pair of us, Mick. Put a bit more wood on that fire will you.

Mick *tosses some bits of an estate agent's sign on the fire and pulls the wardrobe over to block the door.*

Mick Will I ever get her back, do you think?

The Head Advice, Mick? You want advice?

Mick Forget I spoke. (*He looks at his watch.*) Twenty past twelve already. (*He thinks.*) Open University.

He switches on the television and settles back on the bed, lighting up two cigarettes, one of which he gives to the **Head**.

Mick Did you ever see anybody roll a seven-skin joint before?

*The **Head** says 'No' as best he can with a cigarette in his mouth.*

Mick   Watch closely so.

Mick *takes out a packet of skins and sets to work.*

Television presenter   The next programme is in the second-year course on biology and will deal with the reproductive system of the African firefly.

The Head (*looking at the screen and dropping his cigarette in shock*)   Get up, ye animal ye! Oh this fellow's a randy wee divil.

Mick   I'll bet you two-to-one he'll drop the hand on that fly on the second leaf.

The Head   Not at all. The one waving her arse in the air crawling down the stem. Twenty pounds says he'll park his shoes under her bed.

They both watch with baited breath.

Mick *and* **The Head** (*wide-eyed*)   Get away!

Lights fade.